Swing Thoughts

Swing Thoughts

The World's Greatest Golfers Share Their Keys to Mastering the Game

DON WADE

CB

CONTEMPORARY
BOOKS

CHICAGO

Library of Congress Cataloging-in-Publication Data

Swing thoughts : the world's greatest golfers share their keys
to mastering the game / [edited by] Don Wade.
　　　p.　　cm.
　　Includes index.
　　ISBN 0-8092-3912-4 (cloth)
　　ISBN 0-8092-3638-9 (paper)
　　1. Swing (Golf)　I. Wade, Don.
　GV979.S9S94　　1993　　　　　　　　　　　　　　92-42263
　　　　　　　　　　　　　　　　　　　　　　　　　　　　　CIP

Interior illustrations by Dom Lupo
Front cover photo by Stephen Szurlej

Published by Contemporary Books, Inc.
Two Prudential Plaza, Chicago, Illinois 60601-6790
Manufactured in the United States of America
International Standard Book Number: 0-8092-3912-4 (cloth)
　　　　　　　　　　　　　　　　　　　0-8092-3638-9 (paper)
10　　9　　8　　7　　6　　5　　4　　3　　2　　1

CONTENTS

Index 212

FOREWORD

Throughout my career I've used a wide variety of swing thoughts or keys, trying to find the ones that will give me improved distance, control, accuracy, or just a better way to deal with tournament pressures. Sometimes these are mental images. Other times they are actual physical keys. These may vary from tournament to tournament and even from day to day. Bob Jones was once asked what was his best swing thought. "Whichever one worked best last," he said.

I believe that swing thoughts, whether they are for the full swing, the short game, or your mental approach to a round, are the secrets to playing your best golf as often as possible. A good key not only will help you establish a swing that will perform best under pressure but also will help you keep your composure during a poor round. Too often I've seen players panic and begin searching for a new key. Once that kind of confusion sets in, they're on their way to a big number. My advice is to grind it out and head for the practice area.

It's also important to remember that you should

focus on one—two at the most—keys for your swing at any one time. It's just not going to work if you have too many thoughts going through your brain for a swing that takes just a couple of seconds. My rule is to keep things as simple as possible.

As you read this book you'll see that different players have come up with a wide variety of keys to solve the same problems—tempo, for example. Some will seem very similar, while others are completely contradictory. That's just the nature of the game.

I believe that all golfers can find something in this book that will help them improve. I know that using swing thoughts works for me. I hope this book works for you.

Tom Kite

PREFACE

When I was a kid, just learning to play the game, I had the uncommon good fortune to have Harold Cahoon, the professional at the Concord (Massachusetts) Country Club, take an interest in me. On summer weekdays when there wasn't much play, I would spend the day shagging balls during his lessons. It was like getting paid to watch and see what worked and what didn't. Harold was always generous with tips, lessons, and advice, and one of his best suggestions formed the basis for this book.

Harold always said that people are creatures of habit, both good and bad, and that was especially true when it came to the golf swing. The chances are, Harold told me, that if you have a flaw in your swing it will never really disappear. When the pressure is on, or when you get a little lazy, the flaw will reappear. The trick is identifying the flaw, recognizing the problem it creates, and having a key to correct it. For example, most of us tend to get quick when the heat is on. To solve this, you need to find a little key that will help you swing with a good tempo. Throughout this book you'll find many different keys to help you do just that . . . and solve many other flaws as well.

Harold also understood that a person's memory is seldom infallible. That's why he urged people to keep a small notebook in their bag that contained reminders of different swing keys that had worked over the years. When their swing began to go south or their short game began to fray, their notebook was always there, reminding them of what had worked before. Oftentimes that was just enough to get them through the round before heading for the practice range to try to work out the problem.

A few years ago I was playing golf with Nancy Crossman, my editor at Contemporary Books and a certifiable golf addict. She was having a problem with her swing, and I mentioned a swing key that had always worked for me. Sure enough, it solved her problem and one of mine as well—what I was going to do for my next book.

I'd like to thank Nancy for doing what she does so well: coming up with fresh ideas and then patiently encouraging her writers to get the most out of them. I'd also like to thank one of the genuinely nice guys in this business, Dom Lupo, for the terrific job he did with the artwork.

This book wouldn't have been possible without the help of the players on the PGA, Senior PGA, and LPGA Tours, who were so generous with their time and ideas over these past few years. In explaining to me what swing thoughts worked best for them, many players were able to relate them to specific tournaments, and these are noted in the book. In other cases, the thoughts were more general— thoughts the players had used on and off over the years—and in these instances, they are not tied to any specific tournament.

Will every one of these keys work for you? I doubt it, but I'm confident that all can come away from this collection with at least a few tips that will help shave a few strokes off their card.

Finally, I'd like to thank Harold Cahoon for taking the time to get a young kid interested in the game of golf. It meant more than he ever knew.

Don Wade

PART I
FULL-SWING
THOUGHTS

TOM PURTZER
THE 1988 SOUTHWEST CLASSIC

LET YOUR UPPER BODY
CONTROL YOUR TURN

I've always played my best golf when I've been able to focus on one good swing thought rather than getting confused with a lot of different things to try to remember. Once you find a thought that you can trust, it allows you to put your game on cruise control, because you don't have any doubts or indecision about your swing. You can just feel free to go ahead and hit the shots you need to hit.

Coming into the 1988 Southwest Classic, I had been trying to find a way to improve the timing of my turn. I had been inconsistent, and sometimes my arms would swing too fast. Other times my hips would get out ahead, and I'd sort of spin out.

I found that if I concentrated on leading my backswing by turning my belt buckle around to the right and then turned my belt buckle toward my target on the downswing, it dramatically improved the timing and pace of my swing. It's very easy to swing too quickly when you let your arms set the pace of your swing, but by keying my swing to my upper-body turn, I was able to swing at a consistently good tempo.

This key works especially well under pressure, when your swing naturally tends to get fast. I know it really helped me in this particular tournament, when I was able to beat Mark Brooks in a playoff.

RUSS COCHRAN
THE 1991 CENTEL WESTERN OPEN

TAKE THE CLUB BACK VERY SLOWLY

We all have weaknesses or tendencies in our games that we have to guard against, especially under pressure. It's the same whether you're a pro with a chance to win a tournament or a weekend player standing on the first tee in front of your friends. The trick is finding a key that will help you perform under that pressure.

I tend to be a nervous, anxious player in the first place, so I've found that if I just think about taking the club back away from the ball very slowly it helps focus my attention and improves the pace of my swing.

In the 1991 Western Open it came down to me, Freddie Couples, and Greg Norman in the last round. I knew that to win I would have to get everything out of my game, because Freddie and Greg are just so talented. There was a lot of pressure on the first tee, but once I got that hole under my belt things sort of settled down through the middle of the round. I just concentrated on doing the same thing before every shot and making a slow move away from the ball.

The last third of the round was very difficult. The closing holes at Cog Hill are pretty tough to begin with, and with the wind blowing around 35–40 miles per hour it really forced me to concentrate on every shot. As it turned out, Greg and Fred ran into some problems on the back nine, which gave me a little breathing space, but I know that one simple key—taking the club back slowly—made all the difference for me.

ROCCO MEDIATE
THE 1991 DORAL RYDER OPEN

TURN, TURN, TURN

I've worked a lot with my friend and coach, Rick Smith, on simplifying my game so that when I'm under pressure I can visualize the shot I want to hit and then trust my instincts and muscle memory to allow me to hit it. I really believe that overthinking prevents me from playing my best golf.

The first thing Rick and I worked to develop is a good, consistent preshot routine. If you watch a good free-throw shooter in basketball, you'll notice that he does the same thing before every shot. He'll bounce the ball the same number of times, focus on the front rim, and then, when he's comfortable, he'll take his shot. If you watch the best golfers, you'll see that they do the same thing too. Jack Nicklaus is the perfect example of this, and if it's good enough for Jack, I guess it's good enough for the rest of us.

My key swing thought, especially when I'm under pressure, is to "turn, turn, turn." I concentrate on making as big a turn as I comfortably can on my backswing and then turning back through the hitting area. But the key is really the backswing, because if you don't turn back, you can't turn through and get the most out of your swing.

When I won at Doral, I kept reminding myself to swing with what I call "good speed." In other words, what I wanted to avoid was getting too fast, which usually causes me to end my backswing too soon. If your last thought before you take the club away from the ball is one that will help you swing with a good tempo, I think you'll find you're in pretty good shape.

JODIE MUDD
THE 1990 PLAYERS CHAMPIONSHIP

COORDINATE YOUR ARMS
WITH YOUR LOWER BODY

For a swing thought to be really effective, it has to be something that helps you overcome a flaw or weakness in either your swing or your game. I tend to get too fast with my lower body. As a result, when my timing is off, I sometimes hang back and hook the ball or hang left and hit a big slice. As a result I'm not always a very straight driver, so it's a problem I'm constantly working on overcoming.

Coming into the Players Championship at Sawgrass, I was focusing on coordinating my arm speed and my leg action, trying to get my timing in a good sequence. It worked pretty well for the first three rounds, but I knew the real test would come on Sunday.

My thought going into the last round was just to slow things down and keep my knees flexed. I've found that as long as my knees are flexed it's easier to keep my swing together. In fact that one thought carried me through the last four, crucial holes. I can remember standing on the 17th tee, looking at that green surrounded by water, reminding myself to keep my legs flexed and swing at a good pace. I pushed the ball slightly but remained in control until the end.

LARRY MIZE
THE 1987 MASTERS

MOVE THE BALL FORWARD FOR HIGHER, SOFTER SHOTS

People always talk about what an advantage power is at Augusta National, and that's certainly true. Just look at the players who have been the most successful at the Masters: Sam Snead, Ben Hogan, Jimmy Demaret, Arnold Palmer, Jack Nicklaus, Tom Watson, and Seve Ballesteros. Those are all players with tremendous strength.

But as important as power is at Augusta, it also helps if you can hit high, soft approaches to the greens, because it's vital that you land the ball in certain spots to leave yourself makable putts or—and this is almost as important—avoid three-putts or worse.

On the practice tee I was experimenting with different things I could do to get the ball up a little higher. I found that if I moved the ball slightly forward in my stance, my iron shots got up in the air a little quicker and, more importantly, I could make a slightly more aggressive swing with my driver without worrying that I'd hook the ball. I didn't try to kill the ball, just gradually accelerate the clubhead through the hitting area. As a result I was driving the ball about 265–270 yards, which is 10 or 15 yards longer than usual. That meant I could hit at least one club less into the greens, which is a tremendous advantage because the greens were even firmer than usual that year. It also allowed me to go at the par 5s in two, which is the key to scoring well at Augusta.

In the final round I hit a good drive on 18 that left me with just a 9-iron into the green. I made the birdie, which gave me a lot of confidence going into the playoff with Seve and Greg Norman. Seve went out with a bogey on 10, and then on 11 I chipped in from the right side for a birdie.

TED SCHULZ
THE 1991 NISSAN LOS ANGELES OPEN

STICK WITH THE SHOT THAT WORKS BEST

All good players have a shot that they're most comfortable with. Some guys like to hit the ball left to right, while others prefer to draw the ball.

For a long time I tried to hit every shot pretty much straight, but I was just too inconsistent. Back at the 1989 Doral, I decided to go with a fade, which was the shot that I was more comfortable with under pressure. Once I decided to play that way, I made a commitment to give it a fair test, and it's worked out pretty well.

The first thing I do as I study the shot I'm facing is to try to get an image of what it's going to look like. Then I aim slightly left of my target and hit a little fade or block. The key is concentrating on not letting my left wrist break down until well after impact.

Because this is basically the only shot I try to play, I have a lot of confidence in my ability to pull it off, no matter how much pressure I'm under. Just having that confidence can help you pull off a tough shot. I admit that when I do have to try to hook the ball I don't do as well, but I think it's a good trade-off. I know that it certainly worked for me at Riviera, which is one of the toughest courses we play all year—and if it worked there, I'm willing to take my chances anyplace else.

JANE GEDDES

The 1986 Women's Open

SWING FROM *A* TO *B* UNDER PRESSURE

I think the secret to any swing thought is to keep it as simple as possible. When you are playing poorly or under a lot of pressure, you don't want to have to worry about anything too complicated or cosmic.

My best swing key has always been to think to myself, "*A* to *B*, back and through," and to swing at that pace. I'll actually say it quietly to myself to reinforce the thought. It's a good key for every shot, from the driver through the bag to the putter.

Coming to the last hole of the Women's Open at NCR in Dayton, Ohio, I knew I was close to the lead but didn't realize I was tied with Sally Little. The 18th isn't a long hole, which was the good news, but the landing area was very tight. There's a bunker on the right side and mounds on the left. I wanted to take the trouble out of play, so I hit a 3-wood off the tee, which left me a good 5-iron into the green. I got my par, which set up a playoff the next day, which I won.

When I think back on the Open, the other thing that stands out in my mind is how many times over the years I'd be practicing and I'd say, "OK, this is the 72nd hole of the Open." I'd try to imagine what the pressure would be like and then go ahead and try to hit a good shot. Of course, there's no way you can really practice under that kind of pressure, because until you've been there you can't imagine what it's like. Still, for weekend golfers who get first-tee jitters it might help if you said to yourself, "This is the first tee this Saturday. Here's the shot I want to hit." And then go ahead and try to hit the shot. For that matter, you should always have a thought or goal in mind for every ball you hit. Otherwise you're not really practicing; you're just beating balls.

DONNA ANDREWS
THE 1992 U.S. WOMEN'S OPEN

CONCENTRATE ON BALANCE AND TEMPO

For the three weeks leading up to the 1992 Women's Open at Oakmont, I worked very hard on my balance and tempo. All that work paid off with a third-place finish and a lot of confidence.

I try to make sure that my weight is centered evenly over my feet, not out on my toes, which is a tendency I have to guard against. If I can keep my weight centered, I very rarely find myself out of balance at the end of the swing. I also concentrate on keeping my knee flex constant throughout the entire swing. When I set up to the ball, I want to feel as though I'm sitting on a barstool with my feet firmly planted on the ground. I want to be in the same position through impact.

In terms of tempo I sometimes think "1-2" to myself when I'm practicing both full shots and around the greens, but once I get on the course I try to establish the tempo of my swing with my practice swing. A good tempo is also important because it helps me keep all the parts of my body—my arms,

legs, and upper body—connected throughout the swing. That's tough to do when you're swinging out of your shoes.

Good balance and a good tempo are especially important if you hit the ball into the rough, which is very high and thick at the Open. There's a natural tendency to swing harder than usual when you're in the rough. When you do that, it's very easy to ruin both your tempo and balance—and hit a lot of ugly shots.

MIKE REID
THE 1988 NEC
WORLD SERIES OF GOLF

THINK SLOWLY, MOVE SLOWLY,
AND SWING SLOWLY

My father was a great fan of Julius Boros, and so it was only natural that when I was learning to play I was a fan of his, too. One of the things that impressed me about his game was how relaxed he always seemed. He did everything slowly: he ate slowly, he drove to the course slowly, he walked slowly, and he made a swing that appeared almost effortless. The only thing he did quickly was hit the shot. He didn't waste any time.

As a result, my game is dominated by rhythm and timing. I know it's important for me to take my time if I'm going to play well. In fact my caddie will often remind me to keep it slow, and not just with my swing. It starts with how I walk up to my ball, pull the club from the bag, set up to the ball, and begin the swing. Everything has to be done with a nice, smooth tempo. If I get quick in any one part of my game, it upsets the rhythm of my entire game.

The other thing that I really pay attention to is my breathing. Very often, when you get under pressure, you tend to take a lot of shallow breaths, which reduces the amount of oxygen to your system and short-circuits your brain. You just can't think as clearly as you need to under the stress of competition. To guard against this, I really pay attention to how I'm breathing. This was particularly true in the 1988 World Series at Firestone, when I wound up in a playoff with Tom Watson and was able to win it with a par on the first extra hole.

STEVE PATE
THE 1991 HONDA CLASSIC

DON'T FORGET YOUR PRESHOT ROUTINE

One of the biggest differences between good players and higher handicappers is in the way they approach playing a shot.

The good player has a specific routine that he or she goes through for every shot played, while the higher handicapper often does something different every time. This is especially important under pressure, which was the case for me when I won down at the Honda.

On any full shot I stand behind the ball, facing the target, and pick a spot about 12 inches in front of the ball to aim at. It can be an old divot, a light piece of grass, or anything else that's easily noticeable. Then I move into my address position, placing the clubface behind the ball and building my stance around it.

Too often amateurs make the mistake of taking their stance and then putting the clubhead behind the ball, which often leads to shots that are missed because they are misaimed. After I've taken my stance, I always take two waggles and then hit it. No more, no less.

On the greens I follow the same routine except I take just one practice stroke and then concentrate very hard on not looking up until after I've struck the putt.

MARK BROOKS
THE 1988 SAMMY DAVIS JR.
GREATER HARTFORD OPEN

SET THE CLUB
AT THE TOP OF YOUR BACKSWING

I think most players have to guard against getting quick and not making a good, full backswing, especially under pressure. I know it's something I have to concentrate on, and I did when I won at Hartford in 1988.

A lot of different swing thoughts will help you complete your backswing, but the one that works best for me is concentrating on setting the club at the top of my backswing. It's almost as though there was a slot over my right shoulder that I'm trying to put my hands into.

The beauty of this thought is that it is so simple and yet it does two crucial things: first, it helps you complete your backswing; second, it helps set a good tempo for your swing, because you just naturally will take the club back slowly.

DAVIS LOVE III
The 1991 MCI Heritage Classic

MAKE SURE YOU'RE COMFORTABLE WITH THE SHOT

When I'm playing well, I usually find a swing key or, at the most, two when I'm warming up on the practice tee before my round. Then, hopefully, I can just go out there and play, going through my routine before every shot and basically just trusting my swing.

But in almost any round you're going to face difficult or unusual shots, and very often the difference between winning and losing is in your ability to pull off these shots to save par. That was the situation I faced on the 16th hole at Harbour Town in the final round of the 1991 Heritage.

I had to hit a low 5-iron that needed to hook about 30 yards around a big tree and then run onto the green. It was a difficult shot, because anytime you have to hit a shot that hooks that much you run the risk of it getting away from you. It was crucial that I get myself comfortable with the shot, and to do that I took several practice swings, visualizing

the shot and making a swing that would produce the shot I needed. After about five or six practice swings I went ahead and hit the shot. It came off perfectly. Again, the key when you're facing a tough or unusual shot is to give yourself a good chance at becoming comfortable with it—and to do that, make plenty of practice swings.

PAT BRADLEY
WORK FOR EXTENSION ON THE BACKSWING

Ten years ago I began working with Gail Davis on my swing, and she made one important change that has really helped my career.

I have a tendency to get very upright with my swing, and when that happens I don't make much of a turn, I hang left, and I hit a lot of weak shots out to the right.

My one real swing thought—the one I use week in and week out—is to make sure I can feel my left shoulder stretch on the backswing. I know that if I can feel that muscle stretch I've made a good turn and am swinging on a correct plane. There's one other plus to this swing key: if I concentrate on feeling my left shoulder stretch on the backswing, it means I'm completing my backswing and am swinging with a good tempo. If you have a problem with your tempo, I think this key can really help you a lot.

BILLY ANDRADE
THE 1991 KEMPER OPEN

GUARD AGAINST GOING LEFT

I've always been a pretty accurate player, but every so often I'd hit a big, hard hook and get myself in all kinds of trouble. That happened on the 13th and 15th holes at the 1991 Memorial Tournament. After my round I went to the practice tee with my pro, Rick Smith, and we came up with a way to protect against losing the ball to the left.

The first thing I do is open my stance and aim about 10 yards left of my target. Most people play their short irons from an open stance anyway, so it's not that big an adjustment, and I think it helps you see the target and visualize the shot better than you can from a closed stance. Hitting the ball with a fade like this helps you get the ball up into the air easier, which is a big help when you need to stop the ball on the green. I also think this makes it easier to make a good, full turn.

When I'm actually hitting the shot, my one thought is to concentrate on keeping my left arm and wrist firm through the hitting area. This allows me to swing as hard as I want without worrying about hitting a hook. At the very worst I'll hit the ball straight and miss my target just to the left, but not by much.

When you look at the guys who play like this—Jack Nicklaus, Lee Trevino, Bruce Lietzke, and Freddie Couples just to name a few—you can see that they are all very good drivers, and they're not short hitters either.

By eliminating the danger of a hook, I've been able to develop a lot more confidence in my ball striking, which just naturally puts you in a better frame of mind. Now I feel like I can go ahead and play aggressively, and if I make a few putts in the course of the week, I'll have a good shot at winning. That was how I was thinking when I won the 1991 Kemper, and it carried over the following week when I won at Westchester.

I think this is a particularly good tip for most weekend players because they have a tendency to be too closed at address, especially with their shoulders. A good way to check this is to have a friend stand behind you when you address the ball and see where your shoulders, hips, and feet are pointed. If they are parallel to or left of the target line, you're OK, but if they aim to the right you might try playing from a more open stance.

TURN

TILT

PAUL AZINGER
THE 1987 PHOENIX OPEN

TURN, DON'T TILT

It seems like I've had a different swing thought in every tournament I've won, but the most consistent key has been to concentrate on making a level swing. I have a tendency to tilt my left shoulder down on the backswing, which more than likely leads to a swing that is too steep. It also leads to sliding back and forth in my swing rather than making a good, tight turn.

I've found that if I try to keep my shoulders level throughout the swing, I make a much better turn and hit the ball a lot more consistently. The best example was on the last hole in the 1987 Phoenix Open, my first tour win.

The hole is a par 4 with water left and a bunker to the right. I had a one-shot lead over Hal Sutton, and was probably as nervous as I've ever been in my life. Standing on the tee, I reminded myself to turn and not tilt. I hit a good drive and a 7-iron to 20 feet. It wasn't the first time that key worked for me, but it was the most important.

SAM SNEAD

MY COURSE-RECORD 60 AT THE LOWER CASCADES

EXTEND YOUR ARMS THROUGH THE BALL

One afternoon, back in 1983, I was watching a baseball game on television, and a player said that he had shaken his hitting slump by extending his arms through the hitting area. Well, I had been in a slump of my own, and this hit me like a ton of bricks. I realized I had been cutting my swing off and not getting much zip on the ball.

The next day I went to the Lower Cascades course at the Homestead to play with some friends of mine. I concentrated on making sure I extended my arms through the ball and went out in 30 strokes, including 13 putts. I had another 30 on the back, and it would have been a 29 if I hadn't got a bad break on the last hole, when my approach shot took a crazy bounce. I wanted that 59 so bad I could taste it.

What made the 60 even sweeter was that it tied the record set by my nephew, J.C. It proves that sometimes the best things in golf come where you least expect them.

LYNN CONNELLY
THE 1991 INAMORI CLASSIC

COMPLETE YOUR SWING

Like a lot of players, I have a tendency to get short and quick with my backswing, especially under pressure or when I'm not playing very well.

In the 1991 Inamori Classic near San Diego I just sort of chunked it around in the first three rounds, although I made a lot of good saves in the third round and shot a 68, which left me four shots behind Laura Davies and Robin Walton.

Following the round I went to work with Gardner Dickinson, trying to work out the problems in my swing, which had gotten both short and quick. He told me not to think of anything but getting my left shoulder under my chin on the backswing. All of a sudden the feeling kicked in. It freed up my swing, making it longer and slower and giving me time to get back into the ball. It also kept the tension out of my smaller muscles by relying on a good turn of the big muscles in my upper body.

I couldn't believe how much confidence I had going into the final round. I wasn't worried about my mechanics because I knew I was swinging well. I just went out and played the course, shooting a 67. Laura shot a 67 too, so I couldn't catch her, but I wound up tied with Judy Dickinson for second place and picked up a good check.

LYNN CONNELLY
THE 1991 J.C. PENNEY
MIXED TEAM CLASSIC

KEEP YOUR HEAD BEHIND THE BALL

I have a tendency to slide ahead of the ball on the downswing, which can cause me to block the ball or occasionally hit a big hook. Before the tournament I started to work on keeping my head behind the ball through impact. To help ensure that I did this, I'd cock my head to the side before starting my swing.

Not only did this help prevent me from sliding my body ahead of the ball, but it also helped keep my swing centered throughout the shot, which greatly improved my ball striking. My partner, Buddy Gardner, and I opened with a 67 that left us three shots off the lead, but we followed that with rounds of 69-67 and closed with a 65 that left us out of a playoff that was won by Billy Andrade and Kris Tschetter.

AMY ALCOTT
The 1980 U.S. Women's Open

THINK "1-2-3" UNDER PRESSURE

In 1980 the Women's Open was played at Richland C.C. in Nashville, Tennessee. The heat and humidity were incredible, with temperatures over 100 degrees each day. The biggest challenge was keeping your concentration from one shot to the next.

Early in my career I learned that if I concentrate on tempo, especially under pressure, I hit the ball better than if I try to concentrate on some mechanical key. My secret to good tempo is swinging to a "1-2-3" count. I've always admired Sam Snead's swing, and it always looked like there was a distinct "1-2-3" count to his swing.

On the count of "one" I make a slight forward press with my hands and right knee. At the top of my backswing I count "two," and then on "three" I hit through the ball, reaching for the sky and making a good, high finish.

At the Women's Open, when my mind began to wander and I was losing my concentration over the

① ② ③

ball, I forced myself to actually count "1-2-3" to myself as I hit the shot. It focused my attention on the shot at hand and also helped me swing with a good tempo. What else could you ask from one little swing thought?

BRUCE FLEISHER

THE 1991 NEW ENGLAND CLASSIC

REMEMBER HOGAN'S PANE OF GLASS

I come from the old school of golf instruction, and throughout my career I've greatly admired the theories of Ben Hogan. In fact, when I left the tour and got a job as a teaching professional, I based my work on many of the principles Hogan put forth in his books.

One area of instruction that I've focused on, both in my own game and in my teaching, is the rotation of the upper body and the importance of keeping the club swinging on the correct plane. This is particularly important in the hitting area, which I define as the area from the right hip to the left hip.

In Hogan's book *Five Lessons*, he presented one of the clearest images I've ever seen to help golfers swing the club on the correct plane. He suggested imagining a pane of glass sitting on an angle upward from the ball through the shoulders. The idea is that in no point in the swing should the clubhead move outside the plane, or it will break the pane of glass.

Rotating my arms under this imaginary pane of glass is the most important swing thought I have, because I know that if I do this the club will automatically square up at impact. Most of the time when I see people swinging on the wrong plane, they either move the club outside the plane on the backswing or swing the club too far to the inside of the line and then reroute the clubhead at the top of the swing and come over the top on the downswing—resulting in either a shot that's pulled to the left or a slice. Either way, the pane of glass is broken.

I think of this key on every shot except for pitching or putting, and it's particularly important when I'm facing a tight driving hole or have a shot to a difficult pin placement.

The 17th hole at Pleasant Valley C.C., site of the 1991 New England Classic, is an excellent example. It's a 420-yard par 4 and probably the best hole on the course. If you're going to choke, this is a hole that makes it very easy. If you drive the ball down the right side, you're dead, but the left side isn't a true bailout either. The long hitters can hit a fairway wood or a 1-iron for position, but I have to hit a driver to give myself the best chance on the approach shot, which is over water.

I came to the 17th in the last round paired with Morris Hatalsky. I was one shot behind the leaders, who were four or five holes back. I knew I had to hit a good drive to have any chance at winning. I felt very focused and hit a big drive, followed by a good 9-iron. I came off with a par but birdied the last hole to tie for the lead, then won the playoff with Ian Baker-Finch.

MARK HAYES
USING A KEY
TO MAKE A SWING CHANGE

When I was a student at Oklahoma State University, Labron Harris, Sr., the golf coach, taught me a swing that was fairly common in those days. You tried to "get underneath the ball" by swinging very much from the inside and delaying your release for as long as possible. When my timing was right, this worked very well, but only for short periods of time. I was able to win three times, but I knew my swing wouldn't hold up. Eventually I'd begin hanging back too much on the downswing, and because there was so much lateral movement on the downswing I'd wind up in the classic "reverse C" position at the finish of my swing, which wasn't doing my back very much good.

The other problem with this type of swing is that it has a tendency to break down under pressure because it's only natural to get tight and quick when you are under the gun. For this swing to really work, you need to make a strong release at impact, and that didn't always happen, especially when I began to lose some confidence in my swing.

Today teaching has changed and people have an entirely different concept of the golf swing. Instead of trying to swing under the ball, today my mental image is one of trying to cover the ball with my right side. Curtis Strange is a very good example of this type of swing.

Today my key image is a simple one: when I am halfway through my downswing, at the point where the shaft is vertical to the ground and parallel to my body, I want to feel as though my left shoulder is level with, or just slightly lower than, my right shoulder. In my old swing, in the same position, my left shoulder would be much higher than my right because I was trying to swing so much more from the inside. I think this new swing is a lot more repeatable, consistent, and forgiving than my old swing. I know it's starting to pay dividends now.

ANDY NORTH
The 1978 and 1985 U.S. Opens

MAKE A "FRAME-BY-FRAME" SWING FOR BETTER TEMPO

Because of my height (6'4"), my overriding concern is tempo. If I can keep my swing smooth and under control, I can get away with murder. Like anyone, I go through a lot of different day-to-day swing thoughts, but when I'm playing in a tournament my biggest thoughts concern how to swing with a good rhythm.

I've found that a good mental image is a metronome. I try to visualize my arms moving at a nice, slow "1-2" pace—the slowest tempo I can possibly imagine. Another thought that works very well is visualizing my swing as though it were being played back on a VCR, frame by frame, almost in stop-action. I actually try to swing back and down as though my swing were a series of freeze-frames, because it helps my tempo so much, particularly at the top of my swing, when I make the transition from the backswing to the downswing.

These keys helped me in both my U.S. Open

wins. At Cherry Hills in 1978, I led by four strokes with five holes left to play. The pressure was unlike anything I'd ever experienced, and I struggled over those last few holes, eventually coming to 18 needing a bogey to win by a shot over J. C. Snead and Dave Stockton. I hit my drive into the right rough, guarding against the pond that is on the left side of the hole. My 8-iron second shot came up just short of the left-hand bunker, and then I came up just short with my third shot, putting it in the sand. Now I had to get up and down to win the Open, and the wind was blowing about 30 miles an hour. I just concentrated on making a smooth swing and accelerating the clubhead through the sand. The ball landed four feet from the hole, and I made the putt. Throughout those closing holes, when I could have easily let the championship slip away, I constantly reminded myself to swing with a smooth tempo, and it helped me hold my round together.

The same thing happened at Oakland Hills in 1985, when I won my second Open. In the final round I hit the ball all over the lot on the first 11 holes. On 12, I drove the ball into a fairway bunker on the right side. It was a cold, dreary day, and it would have been very easy to lose my concentration at that point. Instead I told myself that I still had a chance if I could just hold it together, since I was either tied for the lead or just a shot back.

The 12th hole is a 568-yard par 5 that doesn't offer much room for error. As I stood over my difficult 5-iron bunker shot, I concentrated very hard on making the slowest, smoothest swing I could. The shot came off perfectly, leaving me with just a wedge into the green. I made my par and went on to win by one shot over Dave Barr, T. C. Chen, and Denis Watson.

TOM WEISKOPF
THE 1968
ANDY WILLIAMS–SAN DIEGO OPEN

KNOW YOUR SWING—AND YOURSELF—
UNDER PRESSURE

The one thing you have to know is your swing and what your tendencies are under pressure. For me, everything sped up, so I concentrated very hard on my tempo. I focused on making a complete shoulder turn, because if I did that, I knew I wouldn't pull or hook the ball.

Tempo also entered into my thinking and execution. When I was in a position to win, my mannerisms and thinking would seem to speed up, so I would try deliberately to slow everything down. I'd walk slower, pull the club slower, and even think slower. You don't want to rush into any decisions.

The other thing you must do is eliminate the negatives. If you are a complete player, you must try to hit the proper shot, whether it's shaping the shot you need to hit a fairway or playing the percentage shot to a difficult pin. Once you've visualized the shot you need to hit, you can't back off or second-guess yourself. If you do, you've got almost no chance of hitting a good shot.

The last thing I think about on any shot is getting good extension through the shot. You can't just hit and hope. My key was to always extend my hands directly at my target for as long as possible. This would protect against cutting my swing off under pressure.

I'll never forget my first win, at Torrey Pines in the 1968 Andy Williams–San Diego Open. I came to the 72nd hole tied with my playing companion, Al Geiberger, and Raymond Floyd, who was already in the clubhouse.

The last hole at Torrey Pines is a reachable par 5 for long hitters. The only difference between today and 1968 is that a pond has been added in front of the green.

As I came to the tee, I remember having a clear assessment of the situation. I needed a birdie to win outright, and I also knew that Al wasn't long enough to reach the green in two. For him to make a birdie, he'd have to pitch the ball pretty close, which was not unlikely because he was a great pitcher of the ball.

I had been hitting the ball very solidly all day, so

all I wanted to do was make sure I kept the ball in play. The fairway sloped from right to left in the landing area, so I wanted to start the ball down the right side with a draw. I just tried to make a good turn and swing with a smooth tempo. I just killed the drive, leaving myself 215 yards into the green.

The drive took a lot of pressure off, because I had done exactly what I needed to do. Now, facing a 3-iron shot, I felt very confident because long irons were my strong suit. The pin was cut in the back of the green, so I didn't want to go over the green. I hit a high, soft shot that stopped 25 feet from the hole. Al pitched up to eight feet. All I was trying to do was lag my putt up close, but sometimes you get lucky. It dropped, and I had my first win on tour. I had hit two very good shots and made a putt, but the key was being aware of the situation on the tee and hitting the drive I needed to hit to make everything else possible.

TERRY JO MYERS
THE 1988 MAYFLOWER CLASSIC

SEE AN EXPLOSION OFF THE TEE

When I get on the tee and put the peg in the ground, I try to draw a blank. The driver is one of my strengths, so I have a lot of confidence. I don't really need a mechanical key. My mind already knows how the shot is going to go, so as I stand over the ball I try to imagine an explosion. I try to just see the ball explode as I hit it. It was something I developed on my own one day on the practice tee. I was trying to simulate tournament pressure and then find a way to deal with it. That's how I came up with the explosion image. I'm not sure exactly why it works, but it does, and it certainly worked when I won the Mayflower Classic. It was my first win, and coming down the last nine dueling Amy Alcott and Ayako Okamoto there was a lot of pressure. I hung in there and shot a 71 in the last round to win by a shot.

GEORGE BURNS III
THE 1985 BANK OF BOSTON CLASSIC

POINT THE END OF THE CLUB
AT THE BALL AND THE DIVOT

Throughout my career I've had to protect against hitting a big hook under pressure, and like most other players, I also have a tendency to swing too quickly when the heat is on.

When I won the 1985 Bank of Boston Classic at Pleasant Valley C.C. in Sutton, Massachusetts, I was able to guard against getting too fast and hooking the ball by using a swing thought that stemmed from a drill Jim Flick gave me.

Jim suggested that I try to point the butt end of the club at the ball when my hands were about waist high, on both my backswing and my downswing. Then after I had hit the ball, the shaft should be pointing at the divot when my hands were again waist high.

By using this swing thought I was able to move through the ball without hooking, and it also helped me get plenty of width to my swing. I hit 55 greens that week—and when you hit that many, you're going to give yourself a good chance of winning.

JIM SIMONS
The 1978 Memorial Tournament

VISUALIZE YOURSELF
IN TWO KEY POSITIONS

Even though I had a pretty good amateur career (All-American in 1971 and 1972, 1971 Walker Cup team, low amateur in the 1971 and 1972 U.S. Opens) and won three times on tour, I never really understood the swing until I went to work with Jimmy Ballard. He stresses the importance of staying connected throughout the golf swing, and I found that the best way for me to stay connected was to try to visualize and imagine how I should look and feel at two key positions in my swing: at the top of my backswing and at the finish of my swing.

Using these two images worked very well on the last nine holes at the 1978 Memorial. Muirfield Village is such a demanding golf course, and the pressure of being in contention is so great, that it would have been easy to get carried away and let the situation get out of hand. I found that getting a mental picture of where I wanted to be in these two key positions—and actually trying to feel what those positions should feel like—helped take some of the pressure off and allowed me to make some good swings down the stretch.

DEBBIE MASSEY
The 1990 Mazda Japan Classic

LET YOUR ARMS HANG NATURALLY
TO FIGHT TENSION

When I got to the tournament, I had my basic "jet lag swing" going, which is not the swing you want if you have any thoughts of winning. I could feel a lot of tension and tightness in my hands, arms, and shoulders, and there was no way I could seem to get comfortable over the ball, much less make any kind of swing I could repeat successfully.

Then I discovered that if I lowered my hands and let my arms just hang naturally, the tension disappeared and I felt 100 percent more comfortable over the ball. I was balanced throughout the swing, had a lot better pace, and could repeat the swing time after time. All this made sense, because I use clubs that are two degrees flat to begin with. What had happened was that I had managed to work myself out of position and had been reaching for the ball. This forced me to get my hands out of position, and everything else sort of fell apart from there.

That week my swing held up beautifully. I never felt uncomfortable, and that gave me the confidence to go ahead and shoot at the pins. I shot a 64 in the second round and was 11 under par after three rounds, leading Caroline Keggi and Danielle Ammaccapane by three shots going into the last round, which was rained out.

Just to show you how weird this game is, less than a year later I came to the U.S. Women's Open at Colonial C.C. in Ft. Worth, and I couldn't find the ball. That was particularly frustrating, because the Women's Open is my favorite tournament. It's such a great test of ability and patience.

I was completely mediocre in the first practice round, and things weren't going any better in my second until the fifth hole. I happened to look back down the fairway and saw Betsy King and her teacher, Ed Oldfield. Betsy's address position was perfect, up and over the ball. On the other hand, I had managed to work myself into my old "downhill racer" posture, up and in, over the ball. As soon as I corrected my position and lowered my hands, it was like magic. All of a sudden I was able to let the swing happen instead of trying to make it happen. Once I did that, I was able to enjoy the round and focus on the positives instead of dwelling on the negatives. I was able to become target-oriented instead of worrying about my mechanics. I wound up finishing eighth, which gave me a lot of confidence for the rest of the year.

ED SNEED

The 1982 Michelob Houston Open

START THE SWING WITH YOUR SHOULDERS

In 1975, George Fazio gave me an excellent swing thought. He convinced me that the best way to ensure that I made a good turn and swung the club with a sound tempo was to relax my hands and arms and start the swing with my shoulders. Doing this made it more difficult to get out of my best tempo under pressure.

The other thing that this thought did was promote a lagging of the clubhead away from the ball on the takeaway, which is what Ben Hogan, Sam Snead, and many of the other great players of that era did. This helps guard against breaking off the ball too quickly, which can speed up your swing and often cause you to take the club back too much inside the proper line.

This thought has become so ingrained in my swing that it is basically a fundamental. When I am hitting the ball badly or am under pressure, I find that I even exaggerate the movement of my shoulders, and it seems to help.

In the 1979 Masters, when the pressure became so intense on the final day, I used this thought like a crutch. And while it's true that I didn't win, I executed the shots pretty well. Three years later, at Houston, it did work. I came to the 18th hole tied with Bob Shearer. I hit a pretty good drive, but it found the left rough and I had a bad lie. We both made pars, and then I won the playoff on the first hole.

Another thought that may be useful is for strong players who can control the club. I think they would be better off swinging with a somewhat faster tempo. I know this contradicts a lot of teaching, but I think it makes sense. Under pressure you're going to get faster anyway, so why not ingrain that tempo into your swing? A faster swing has less time for things to go wrong, and it's definitely much better in the wind. It's true that players like Sam Snead and Tom Weiskopf had beautiful long, flowing swings, but there have been some pretty good players with fast swings: Ben Hogan, Tom Watson, Arnold Palmer, and Lee Trevino, just to name a few. The key is, you must be strong enough to control the club throughout the swing.

LARRY NELSON
THE 1983 U.S. OPEN

KEEP YOUR ARMS TOGETHER
THROUGHOUT THE SWING

I've always found that when I get in a pressure situation it's best to have a specific swing key to think of rather than thinking about the situation itself. If you begin dwelling on what's happening around you, it's easy to get distracted.

In the 1983 Open at Oakmont, the most important consideration was keeping the ball in play. The rough at Oakmont was extremely deep and punishing, and the course is guarded by some 200 bunkers, many of them large and severe. If all that wasn't enough, the greens were so hard and fast that you had to be very accurate with your approach shots to have any chance at making birdies. As a result many of the longer hitters rarely hit their drivers that week.

My swing key that week was one that I've often used throughout my career. I try to keep my forearms together throughout my swing. It's as though they are being held together by a big elastic band.

This thought helps ensure that I take the club away from the ball on the correct path and with a good tempo. It also helps guard against becoming disconnected.

I suppose the most memorable hole of the entire tournament was the 72nd. The last hole at Oakmont is a 456-yard par 4. I hit a 3-wood off the tee because the landing area was so narrow and it was crucial that I put the ball in the fairway. I hit the green in two, and while I wound up three-putting for a bogey, it was good enough to beat Tom Watson by one stroke.

LARRY NELSON
THE 1981 PGA CHAMPIONSHIP

SWING AGAINST A FIRM RIGHT LEG

Like many players, I have to guard against making a reverse pivot on my backswing. In other words, instead of shifting my weight to my right side on the backswing, I occasionally have a tendency to hang left on my backswing, particularly with the longer irons and woods.

To protect against this during the 1981 PGA Championship at Atlanta Athletic Club, I keyed on trying to keep my right leg in its address position throughout the swing and then swinging against it. It helped if I thought of my leg as a brace to support my weight as I swung the club back.

My other thought that week was to stay very still over the ball. I found that if I did this it helped keep me from swaying and getting out of position during the swing.

Both of these keys were tested on the closing holes. The 17th is a long par 3, which I hit with a 2-iron and made a par with two putts from 20 feet.

The 18th hole is a dogleg-left 460-yard par 4. The rough was very deep, which made the drive very difficult, and I had to hit the fairway because the second shot was over water to a green guarded by large bunkers. I hit a driver from the tee and then hit a high, soft 4-iron into the green and made a par to beat Fuzzy Zoeller.

ROGER MALTBIE
THE 1976 MEMORIAL TOURNAMENT

STAY IN YOUR FLEX TO FIGHT A HOOK

In early 1976 I was fighting a hook and usually coming out on the losing end of the battle. At Colonial that May, I asked Ken Venturi to look at my swing and give me some advice. Kenny watched me hit some balls and then watched me on the course. He told me the problem was that I was coming out of my knee flex during the swing. This not only caused me to be inconsistent in my ball striking but also caused me to hook the ball.

By keeping my knees flexed during the swing, I was able to swing on a consistent level, which reduced my chances of hitting the ball either thin or fat. And Ken's suggestion that I drive my right knee harder to the left on the downswing helped prevent the clubface from closing too fast, causing me to hook the ball.

For most golfers the true test of how well they are swinging lies in their ability to hit long irons, and at Memorial that test came on the 437-yard par-4 18th, which requires a demanding uphill second shot to a heavily contoured and well-guarded green.

On the 72nd hole of the tournament I hit a very good 4-iron to get me into the playoff with Hale Irwin, which lasted four holes. It ended on 18 when I hit another good 4-iron to set up the win. On both shots I focused on keeping my knees flexed throughout the shot. Of course, a lot of people remember that I kept my chances alive on the 17th hole of the playoff when my approach shot hit a stake that was holding the gallery ropes. The ball kicked back into play, much to Hale's shock and everyone else's amazement, including mine. But heck, I always said I'd rather be lucky than good.

MISSIE BERTEOTTI
THE 1992 WOMEN'S KEMPER OPEN

CONCENTRATE ON YOUR GRIP AND SETUP

Once a tournament starts, I try very hard not to think very much about my mechanics, but early in the week I work very hard on two fundamentals that I think are crucial—my grip and my alignment.

One of the reasons I began playing better early in 1992 was that I realized I was getting out of position at address, with both my grip and my body.

I'd start out with a pretty good grip, but as I set up to the ball and began to waggle the club, I'd work my right hand more and more under the club, into a stronger position. Now I'm very careful about checking my grip, making sure that the V formed by the thumb and forefinger of my right hand is never lower than my right shoulder.

I also discovered that, like a lot of players, I had a tendency to work myself into a more closed position as I set up over the ball. I very rarely see anyone get more open, but a lot of players close up their stance because it feels more powerful.

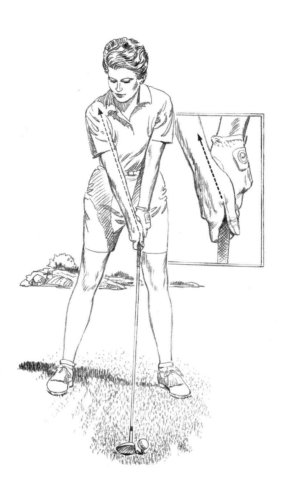

I think it's important to recognize the weaknesses you tend to have in your game, because when you start playing badly you know what to check first, and you also know what to do to solve the problems.

Once you have confidence in your fundamentals it is a lot easier to go ahead and shoot a good number, because you've eliminated that little bit of doubt that holds you back. When I came to Hawaii early in 1992, I had so much confidence that I rarely thought about my mechanics. I just concentrated on the shot I was facing and went ahead and played it with confidence. The result was a second-place finish at the Women's Kemper and a third the following week.

FUZZY ZOELLER
THE 1984 U.S. OPEN

PULL THE HEEL OF THE CLUB INSIDE ON THE DOWNSWING

Swing keys or images work best if you have some physical key to go along with them. In my case, just before I begin my backswing I slide the clubhead away from me so the heel of the club is even with the ball.

This one little move actually does two things: First, it serves as a kind of forward press—a trigger to begin my swing. Some players will move one of their knees toward the ball or slide their hands forward slightly as a way to begin their swing, but this one little move has always worked best for me. The other thing sliding the clubhead out past the ball does is remind me to pull the heel of the club to the inside at the top of my backswing. Doing this helps me guard against coming over the top on my downswing and hitting a big pull-hook.

The test of any swing key is how well it helps you hold up under pressure, and I suppose there's not much more pressure than standing in the fair-

79

way on the last hole of the U.S. Open knowing you have to make a good swing to give yourself a shot at a playoff. That was the situation I was in at the 1984 U.S. Open. I watched Greg Norman hole a huge downhill putt just ahead of me. I thought it was for a birdie that would give him a one-stroke lead, and I began waving my towel in mock surrender. That actually took some of the pressure off. I set up over the ball with a 5-iron and hit a good shot to 20 feet. By then I knew I needed only a par to get into the playoff. I got down in two and won the playoff with a 67 to Greg's 75.

DON POOLEY
THE 1987 MEMORIAL TOURNAMENT

MAINTAIN THE TRIANGLE

I'm 6'2", and like many tall players with long arms I have a tendency to get long and loose with my swing, which results in erratic shotmaking. To combat this, over the years I've tried several keys to help tighten up my swing. I've been most successful when I've concentrated on maintaining the triangle formed by my arms and shoulders for as long as possible on both the backswing and forward swing. On full swings this helps me get plenty of width to my swing without getting out of position. On short shots it helps keep me from getting too wristy, which has helped improve my consistency.

At the Memorial, this particular key gave me the confidence I needed to play aggressively in the final round. I came into the final round trailing Scott Hoch by four shots but closed the gap coming into the final holes. On 17, a 430-yard par 4, I hit an 8-iron to 15 feet and made the putt for a birdie. Then on 18, a 437-yard par 4 that plays to an elevated green, I hit my approach 12 feet from the hole and made another birdie for the win.

On both approach shots I selected a club I could hit hard. When you get in a position to win, or when you feel nervous, I think it's better to take a club and rip at the ball than to try to hit a finesse shot. It just gives you a better margin for error, but it works only if you have confidence in your swing and your ability to pull the shot off.

DON POOLEY
THE 1980 B.C. OPEN

TURN YOUR LEFT SHOULDER
BEHIND THE BALL

When you are under pressure or uncomfortable with your swing, there's a tendency to get short and quick on the backswing. The best key I've found to help me finish my backswing is to turn my left shoulder behind the ball at the top of my swing.

This was the key I used when I won the 1980 B.C. Open at En-Joie G.C. in Endicott, New York. After three rounds I was tied with Lee Trevino at 10-under-par 203. When I came to the 15th hole in the final round, Lee and I were tied with Peter Jacobsen. The 15th is a long, hard par 4 that requires a good drive. Unfortunately I didn't hit one. Instead I drove the ball down the right side, where it hit a tree and dropped straight down, leaving me 235 yards to the green.

At this point in the tournament there was no way I could play safe and lay up, hoping to get up and down for a par. I took a 3-wood and went right at the pin. The ball covered the flag all the way, and when I made the putt it gave me a one-stroke lead, which held up for the next three holes.

HUBERT GREEN
THE 1985 PGA CHAMPIONSHIP

THINK "1-2" ON EVERY SHOT

I've always tried to keep this game as simple as possible, so I guess you could say I'm blissfully ignorant when it comes to things like swing theory and all that stuff. The game is hard enough as it is without getting bogged down with things that are just going to make it harder. Maybe I'm just not a very analytical person in the first place.

The only thing I really ever think about is tempo. My swing isn't going to change too much after all these years, so if I can swing at a tempo that's right for me, then I'll probably be all right. The key is finding the tempo that suits you. I'm a person who does things pretty quickly by nature, so if I tried to swing with Sam Snead's tempo I'd be a wreck.

For some reason just thinking "1-2" when I swing seems to work for me—and it works on every shot, from the driver right down through my putter. I think this is a good tip for golfers of every skill level because it's so simple. When you get under pressure, whether it's the first tee of your local course or in a big tournament like the PGA Championship, you need to get down to basics. The simpler you keep your swing and your thinking, the better off you'll be. That's what I tried to do at Cherry Hills in 1985, when Lee Trevino and I went toe to toe on the last day.

HOLLIS STACY
The 1984 U.S. Women's Open

BE AGGRESSIVE UNDER PRESSURE

When I'm in contention and coming down the final few holes of a tournament, I never play it safe and leave the driver in the bag, because when you try to play safe there's a tendency to steer the ball or hold on and not release the club at impact. When that happens, the tendency is to lose the ball out to the right.

I learned my lesson in the 1981 Moss Creek Women's Invitational, when I tried to play safe in a playoff with Sally Little by hitting a fairway wood off the tee. Naturally I drove it off the earth and handed the tournament to Sally.

Three years later, at the 1984 U.S. Women's Open at Salem C.C. just outside of Boston, I put that lesson to the test on the final hole of the championship.

I began the last round three shots behind Amy Alcott and then doubled the fourth hole to fall seven shots behind. At that point I decided it was about time to get something going. I birdied the fifth and eight holes, then eagled 13 when I holed out a knocked-down 7-iron.

The 18th hole is a difficult par 4. It's a tough driving hole, but I decided to go with a driver and wound up parring the hole and finishing with a two-over-par 290. All I could do was watch and see what Rosie Jones and Amy did on 18. Rosie missed the green with her approach and was too aggressive with her chip, making a bogey. Amy pulled her tee shot into the woods and was blocked out. All she could do was pitch out into the fairway. She missed the green with her approach and wound up double-bogeying the hole to finish third.

It's a funny thing, but the U.S. Women's Open was played in Salem in 1954, the year I was born. Maybe that was a lucky charm for me.

BOB EASTWOOD
THE 1984 USF&G CLASSIC

FOCUS ON YOUR TAKEAWAY

First of all, I work very hard on my address position, because if your setup is wrong it's very hard to hit the ball with any consistency. After I've gotten myself in position, though, my only concern is starting the club away from the ball on the proper plane and at a good tempo.

My key thought is to keep the clubface square to the line for as long as possible. I actually try to visualize the path the club should swing back along. I have a tendency to take the club back too quickly to the inside, which forces me to reroute the club at the top and often leads me to come over the top at the beginning of my downswing.

I worked very hard on this in 1984, when I won the USF&G Classic in New Orleans. I had missed the cut the previous week at Bay Hill, and all I worked on between tournaments was correcting my takeaway. After three rounds I had a two- or three-shot lead, and I began the fourth round with a pair of birdies and was four or five under for the front nine. I was basically on cruise control for the last nine. I missed a few greens, but it didn't matter because I was striking the ball so well my confidence never wavered.

The USF&G was my first win on tour, which meant a lot to me, but winning in Memphis later that year might have been an even bigger win because it proved that winning in New Orleans wasn't a fluke. It also proved that concentrating on my takeaway was a key that would work for me for a long time.

RIK MASSENGALE

THE 1976 SAMMY DAVIS JR.
GREATER HARTFORD OPEN

CLIP THE TEE FROM THE GROUND FOR BETTER DRIVES

When I was a student at the University of Texas, I worked a lot with Harvey Penick, who taught Ben Crenshaw, Tom Kite, and so many other really great players. Mr Penick always stressed the importance of timing and feel and also how important it was to find the bottom of your swing. He always taught me that if I could get my swing to bottom out at the same place, I'd be a lot more consistent shotmaker.

He had a key that's worked for me for a long time. He said that whenever I hit a tee shot I should try to knock the tee out of the ground. On shots from the fairway, the key was trying to just clip the grass under the ball.

In 1976 at Hartford, I came down the stretch in the final round with a one-shot lead over Lee Trevino and Al Geiberger. On the last hole I didn't want to be too conservative, so I took a driver. In situations like this your adrenaline takes over and you lose a lot of feel and muscle memory. My last thought before I took the club was to make sure I clipped the tee out of the ground. This thought helped me stay down through the ball. I hit a good drive and went on to win.

JERRY McGEE

THE 1979 GREATER HARTFORD OPEN

DRIVE YOUR RIGHT
KNEE TOWARD THE TARGET

I've always had extremely good balance, but occasionally I'll fail to finish a swing, and the result is a shot that goes right to right.

A good cure for this is keeping my right knee moving toward the target from the top of my swing until the finish of the shot. The key to making this work is coordinating your leg drive with your upper body, but I've always felt that this one thought helped me get my weight moving through the shot.

If you have a tendency to push a lot of shots, particularly drives, out to the right, this might be a good key for you to work on. Just make a good, full backswing and then begin the downswing by driving your right knee toward the target.

MORRIS HATALSKY
THE 1988 KEMPER OPEN

CONCENTRATE ON YOUR GRIP PRESSURE

Coming into this tournament, I had been fighting my grip for a long time. It just didn't feel quite right, and as a result I couldn't hit the shots I needed to hit under pressure, partially because I was gripping the club too tightly.

Coming into the Kemper, I finally made an adjustment that made my grip feel uniform—that made my hands work together as one. Once that happened, my confidence returned and I was able to grip the club lightly and get rid of the tension in my hands and arms. It also enabled me to swing with my large muscles instead of trying to manipulate the club with the smaller muscles in my hands. As a result, my swings were a lot more consistent.

The final round at Avanel was wild. I went in with a two-shot lead over Craig Stadler, Mike Reid, and John Mahaffey, but the conditions were very difficult, with the wind blowing harder as the day went on. Players were scrambling like crazy. Guys were chipping in and pulling off all kinds of wild shots. I had the kind of round where you don't really have a lot of confidence but you just try to hang on and get what you can out of it.

The 13th hole is a reachable par 5, and I tried to hit the green with a 4-wood. The shot got away from me and went out of bounds. I took a drop and pulled a 3-iron from my bag. I couldn't risk putting another ball out of play, so I was just trying to lay up and limit the damage. This was probably the pivotal shot of the tournament, and there was a lot of pressure. I concentrated on gripping the club as lightly as possible, trying to keep the tension out of my swing. I hit the shot as pure as I possibly could, and the ball wound up on the green. I wound up making a birdie on the second ball, which got me out of the hole with a bogey.

I wound up tied with Tom Kite at 274 and won the playoff on the second hole with a par.

JOHN MAHAFFEY
The 1978 PGA Championship

SLIDE YOUR LOWER BODY
FOR A HIGH, SOFT FADE

Anytime you play in a major championship, you're going to be facing hard, fast greens. That's especially true when the tournament is being played at Oakmont, which has some of the toughest greens I've ever seen.

The best way to deal with greens like this, as well as the narrow fairways and deep rough, is with a high, soft fade. The beauty of this shot is that it will land much more softly than a draw. This lets you shoot at pins you might otherwise play away from. A controlled fade will also help you hit more fairways, which is crucial because if you spend much time in the rough, particularly at a course like Oakmont, you'll be lucky even to make the cut.

I've learned a lot from Lee Trevino during my career, and this shot is one that he's mastered. The key is leading the downswing with your lower body. You want your legs and hips sliding past the ball ahead of the clubhead. Another key is to let your hands lead the clubhead into the ball, making sure that the left wrist doesn't break down at impact. There's no way the ball can go left with this kind of swing.

This swing held up extremely well at Oakmont. At the end of 72 holes I was tied with Tom Watson and Jerry Pate and went on to win the playoff on the second hole of sudden death.

JOHN MAHAFFEY

THE 1986 TOURNAMENT PLAYERS CHAMPIONSHIP

KEEP YOUR RIGHT HEEL DOWN FOR A DRAW

There are some courses that require you to hit a variety of shots to score well. The TPC at Sawgrass is one of them. Everyone always talks about the island green at 17, but that misses the point. The course requires you to be able to fade and draw the ball. It's hard to win here if you can move the ball only one way.

At this stage in my career I had become one-shot dominant. I relied almost exclusively on a fade, and that was fine on most courses, but not at Sawgrass. As a result I worked very hard on finding a way to hit a draw that wouldn't become a snap-hook under pressure.

I found that if I concentrated on keeping my right heel on the ground for as long as possible—almost to impact—I could go ahead and release the club without worrying about a hook.

In any round you can look at the course and

figure out what kind of shot you need to hit to take advantage of how the hole shapes up. When I looked at the tee shot on 18, it was perfect for a draw. A lake guards the entire left side of the hole. If you can start the ball at the center of the fairway and turn it over, you cut a lot of distance off your second shot. That's crucial, because the green is very demanding and it's hard to get the ball close with a long iron.

Larry Mize and I were paired together, and I knew if I could hit a good drive it would put a lot of pressure on him. I hit a perfect draw that left me with just a 6-iron into the green. Larry hung his drive out to the right, guarding against the water. The best he could make was a bogey, and I think it was all set up by my tee shot. It took the pressure off me and put it all on him.

CINDY FIGG-CURRIER
THE 1991 JAL BIG APPLE CLASSIC

REMEMBER MR. PENICK'S
BUCKET OF WATER

I believe that timing is everything in the golf swing. You can have the best mechanics in the world, but without good timing you're never going to be a consistently good ball striker. On the other hand, if you have good timing, you can get away with some swing flaws.

My teacher, Harvey Penick, had a wonderful image to help players develop good timing in their swings. He taught people to imagine they were trying to swing a bucket full of water. If you swing the bucket too fast, the water will spill out on the downswing. The ideal is a slow, pendulumlike swing that almost feels as though you are pausing at the top of the backswing. Doing that helps eliminate any jerky transition from the backswing to the downswing.

At Wykagyl, I was three shots behind Betsy King going into the final round. Wykagyl is an old-fashioned course, with small greens and narrow fairways that require excellent shotmaking. I got off to a horrible start, bogeying four of the first five holes. With that kind of start it's very easy to lose your patience and concentration and get very fast with your swing.

Despite my shaky start, I was able to play the last 12 holes in one under par, mostly because I kept my wits about me and worked to keep a good tempo. The image I had was swinging the club at the same slow pace that I'd use to swing Mr. Penick's bucket of water. It also helps if you remember to keep a good, light grip pressure. If you grip the club too tightly, it's impossible to have any feel for the shots you need to play.

TOM LEHMAN

VISUALIZE YOUR SWING AND SHOT

I'm not really a very mechanical or analytical kind of player. My two main thoughts when it comes to my swing are to stay balanced and swing with a good tempo. I really try to keep things as simple as possible, and I've always figured that as long as you're in good balance throughout your swing you'll be in pretty good shape.

I do think it's important to have a good visual image of both your swing and the shot you're trying to hit. It's as though I have a camera in the back of the ball recording my swing and the ball taking off. Visualizing both my swing and the ball flight helps me focus my concentration just that much better.

DONNA CAPONI
The 1980 Colgate Dinah Shore

GET YOUR LEFT KNEE BEHIND THE BALL

I've always had a very deliberate move away from the ball on the backswing. It's very similar to Nancy Lopez's first move back. In fact, I'm the opposite of most people. I have to guard against getting too slow when the pressure is on. Coming down the closing holes of a tournament, you could read *War and Peace* on my backswing.

The other move I had to guard against was my left knee. Sometimes, under pressure, my knee would move forward on the backswing instead of moving to the right and then back on the downswing. This would cause me to hang left—a classic reverse pivot—and the result would usually be a big, hard hook.

In the 1980 Colgate Dinah Shore I was leading coming to the sixth hole, an excellent par 4. It was very windy, and my lead was only one shot over Amy Alcott, an excellent player in the wind. The sixth was a crucial hole because it was so demanding, both off the tee and with your approach. I hit a pretty good drive into the left center of the fairway. I was left with 185 yards to a pin cut in the back left corner of the green, which meant I had to draw the ball back to the hole. At the same time, I had to make sure the ball didn't get away from me.

I pulled a 5-wood from the bag, and my only thought was to make sure that I made a swing with good pace and that I got my left knee back behind the ball. If I hung left when I was set up to draw the ball, the result would have been a big hook and a big number. I made a good swing, the ball wound up 10 feet from the hole, and I made the putt for a birdie that gave me a little breathing room.

CALVIN PEETE

GET YOUR LEFT THUMB
UNDER THE SHAFT AT THE TOP

When you get under pressure, it's crucial that you make a good, full backswing. My key to ensuring this is really a pretty simple one, but it's one that works, both in practice and in tournaments.

The truth is that when you are playing well you don't really think about anything mechanical. At least I don't. I think a swing key is really something you use when you are trying to groove your swing on the practice tee or in practice rounds or when you are trying to hold it together during a bad round.

The one thing I've worked on is making sure I can feel that my left thumb is under the club and pointed at a point parallel to the target line when I am at the top of my swing. If I can feel that, it ensures three things: First, I'm swinging with a good tempo. If you are swinging too fast, you'll never have the time to feel this sensation. Second, I've completed my backswing. For my thumb to be under the shaft, the shaft has to be pretty close to parallel to the ground. And last, if my thumb is aimed at the point I mentioned, it means the club isn't laid off (pointing to the left of the ideal position) or across the line (pointing to the right of the line).

In each of the 12 tour events that I've won, I've felt that I was performing without thinking about my mechanics. When you are playing well, you don't think too much about your swing. You just think about getting from *A* to *B* and then trying to make a few putts. But to get into this zone, you have to find a way to groove your swing—and that's where a good swing key comes into play.

JIM THORPE
THE 1985 SEIKO-TUCSON MATCH PLAY CHAMPIONSHIP

DON'T GO EASY UNDER PRESSURE

It seems like every time you pick up a magazine or a book about golf, people are being told to swing easy. I disagree. Most people are more likely to swing hard when they are in a pressure situation. I know that's how I am, so what I try to do is think my way around the course to always give myself a shot that I can hit hard.

Here are a few examples: If I have a choice between trying to hit an easy driver or a hard 3-wood from the tee, I'll go with the 3-wood every time, because anytime you try to hit an easy shot with a driver you run the risk of hanging the ball out to the right. The same is true with an approach shot. The last shot I want to leave myself is a 40- to 50-yard wedge into the green. More often than not, when you face that shot, you'll either hit it fat or blade the ball over the green.

When I talk about hitting the ball hard, I don't mean you have to swing out of your shoes. You want to swing in balance and stay within yourself. What you want to avoid is trying to hit a finesse shot when your nerves are working against you.

The 1985 Seiko-Tucson Match Play Championship is a perfect example. Coming into the 15th hole at Randolph Park in Tucson, I had Jack Renner four down with four to play. My caddie, Herman Mitchell, gave me the yardage and told me it was a good 4-iron for me. I knew that with my natural hook, and being as pumped up as I was, I needed to hit a good 5-iron. I aimed about 10 yards right of my target and tried to turn the ball over, drawing it back to the hole. The ball cleared the water in front of the green by 10 yards, and I wound up closing Jack out, 4 and 3.

LEONARD THOMPSON
THE 1990 BUICK OPEN

KEEP YOUR CHEST LEVEL
THROUGHOUT THE SWING

If there's one thing I have to guard against, it's moving up and down during my swing. It's actually a swing flaw I see in a lot of amateurs, but it's not something you ever hear much about. If you make this mistake in your swing, the club never travels on the same path, and as a result your shotmaking is very inconsistent. You'll hit a shot thin one time and then hit the next shot fat.

When I was warming up on the practice tee for the first round of the 1990 Buick Open, I tried to come up with a key that would help keep me steady over the ball. I found that if I picked a spot in the middle of my chest and tried to keep that level through my swing, it kept me from moving up and down, and I hit the ball a lot better.

I went out and shot a 65 to lead the tournament and followed that with a 71 and a 69 to come into the final round trailing Payne Stewart by three shots. It had been 12 years since I won on tour, but

I felt good about my chances because I was hitting the ball so well.

I birdied the first two holes, saved a couple pars, and then birdied 13 and 15. I didn't dare look at a leaderboard, but I knew I must have been close to the lead, so I gambled and hit a driver from the fairway on the 580-yard par-5 16th hole. If it hadn't been the final round, I would have laid up, but I needed to try to make something happen. The ball landed just short of the green. I chipped up to about a foot and took the lead with a birdie.

After I three-putted the 17th, I hit a good drive and then cut a 7-iron into the 18th green that left me with an eight-footer for birdie. I made the putt and then had to wait and see if Payne or Hal Sutton could tie me. They didn't, which was fine with me. I didn't want to face either of those guys in a playoff.

LINE TO TARGET

TOM KITE
THE 1991 INFINITI
TOURNAMENT OF CHAMPIONS

TAKE THE CLUB STRAIGHT BACK

A lot of times the best swing key is one that helps you protect against a weakness or flaw in your swing. I know I have a tendency to take the club back too much to the inside instead of bringing it straight away from the ball. When this happens, I tend to reroute the club at the top of my backswing and come into the ball on an outside swing path. When I do this, anything can happen, but most of the time I'll wind up blocking the ball to the right.

The Tournament of Champions is the first tournament of the year, and naturally you want to play well to get the season off on the right foot. La Costa isn't the kind of course where you can scrape the ball around, make a few putts, and still score pretty well. You just have to be hitting the ball well to have any chance of winning.

Coming into the tournament, I had a swing thought that had some promise. I knew that if I just tried taking the club straight back from the ball it probably wouldn't get the job done. But if I had an image of taking the club back outside the line, it would probably help me take the club straight back from the ball and improve my shotmaking.

I concentrated on this during my practice rounds and when I was on the practice tee, and it really worked great. It's a key that I've used many times since then.

DAVID GRAHAM
THE 1981 U.S. OPEN

STAY WITH YOUR ROUTINE

When people are playing their best golf, they get into a zone where nothing seems to bother them. When this happens, you'll notice that their actions are very repetitive, to the point where they take the same amount of time over every shot. Jack Nicklaus is an excellent example of this.

On the other hand, when players are going badly or get under pressure they're not used to, they get out of their routine and lose all their consistency. At that point, it's all downhill.

When I came into the final round of the Open at Merion, I was extremely confident. I had already won a major championship, the 1979 PGA Championship, so I knew what to expect in terms of pressure. I had been hitting the ball pretty well all week and had been able to handle Merion's difficult greens. I opened with a pair of 68s to trail George Burns by a stroke. On Saturday, I hit the ball like a dream but didn't putt as well as I had in the first two rounds. My even-par 70 left me three back of George.

I went out there thinking about the kind of shots I wanted to play and not worrying about my swing. I'd just walk up to the ball, see the target and the shape of the shot, make sure I was in the proper address position, and then swing away. It certainly helped that I was playing a course that I loved. Merion forces you to think and execute very precisely, rather than just going out and smashing the ball as hard as you possibly can.

I wound up hitting every fairway except the first, which I missed by three feet, and still birdied the hole. Technically, I missed three greens but putted from the fringe on each of them.

My mental state and my routine held up perfectly until the final hole, the 458-yard par-4 18th. I had a two-shot lead over George, and standing on the tee I suddenly got very nervous. The 18th is a very difficult driving hole, since you have to hit the ball over a chasm and through a slender chute.

As I pulled my driver from the bag, my concentration suddenly focused. I remember thinking I had to pick an intermediate target to help me aim. Then I carefully placed the clubhead behind the ball, waggled and got comfortable, then took the club back very slowly and precisely. I absolutely killed the drive—my best of the championship—and I had 184 yards to the front of the green, 202 to the flag from a perfect angle, the left side of the fairway.

George had driven the ball into the right rough and hit a fine second shot, but he got unlucky, and the ball ran through the green and into the thick rough.

As I stood over my ball with a 4-iron, I kept warning myself not to get too excited—there was still golf left to be played. I hit a good shot, with the ball eventually coming to rest 20 feet from the pin. The only way George could catch me was by chipping in. When he didn't, my focus shifted to trying to hole the putt, which would have allowed me to tie Nicklaus's Open record of 272 he set the year before at Baltusrol. My putt trickled over the edge of the cup, and I made the short one coming back for a 67 and a total of 273.

Playing the final hole, when it would have been very easy to become distracted by the situation and the pressure, was the best example I can imagine of the importance of a repetitive routine—and of how important it is to trust your fundamentals and your game.

MARK McCUMBER
THE 1983 WESTERN OPEN

THINK "ROUTINE" UNDER PRESSURE

I don't really have a lot of technical thoughts when I'm playing except that I always try to remind myself to grip the club lightly, especially in tense situations.

The one thing I do concentrate on is my preshot routine, which is something I learned from Bert Yancey. It's something I do over every shot. First I stand behind the ball and study the shot. Next I take three steps as I move into my address position, placing the clubhead down behind the ball. Then I look at my target and adjust my stance, waggle the clubhead, look at the target and adjust my distance a second time, take a third look at the target while I waggle the club one last time, adjust my stance if I need to, then hit the ball.

If I had to pick one tournament where this attention to my preshot routine worked best, it would be the 1983 Western Open. The last hole at Butler National is a long, very difficult par 4 that's guarded by water. I hit a good drive and had a 5-iron left for my second shot. I remember going through my routine very carefully before hitting the shot. I wound up 10 feet from the hole and made the putt for a birdie to win the tournament—my second win on tour.

KEN VENTURI
THE 1964 U.S. OPEN

CLOSE THE GAPS UNDER PRESSURE

I like to visualize two gaps in my swing: the gap between my left shoulder and my chin on the backswing and between my right shoulder and my chin on the downswing.

On the downswing I concentrate on getting my left shoulder to my chin. This ensures not only that I'll make a good, full backswing but also that it will be smooth and slow, since it's almost impossible to move your shoulder fast enough to hurt your tempo.

On the downswing I want to make sure I keep my head down—centered behind the ball—until my right shoulder drives under my chin. This helps me stay down on the shot and also helps keep the clubhead moving toward the target for as long as possible.

In the final round of the 1964 U.S. Open at Congressional C.C. outside of Washington, the heat and humidity were debilitating. I felt very weak and was having a hard time concentrating.

Midway through Saturday's 36-hole final round, my swing began to break down. I needed a swing key to get me back on track and remembered this key that I had been taught by Byron Nelson. It was the only key I had coming down the final stretch of holes. It helped me think "swing" instead of "hit" and also gave me something to concentrate on under the pressure, rather than letting my mind wander.

LANNY WADKINS
THE 1985 LOS ANGELES OPEN

KEEP YOUR HEAD UP
AND BEHIND THE BALL

Over the years I've developed about 12 different swing thoughts that have worked at one time or another. The key is finding the one that works best that week and knowing when to move on to another one, because there's a tendency to overdo things and fall into a bad habit.

I have a tendency, when I'm not swinging very well, to dip down in my swing and let my head slide ahead of the ball, which leads to all kinds of bad shots.

At the 1985 Los Angeles Open I tried focusing on keeping my head level and behind the ball throughout my swing. Whatever the reason, I hit the ball great that week and had the confidence to shoot at pins that were tucked all over the place. I could really play aggressively because I knew that even if I made a bogey I could get it back in a hurry. I wound up shooting a 16-under-par 264, which set the tournament record.

BEN CRENSHAW
THE 1990
SOUTHWESTERN BELL COLONIAL

SWING THE CLUBHEAD

Bobby Jones's wonderful book, *Bobby Jones on Golf*, is the best book I've ever read on actually playing the game. I have it with me whenever I'm playing in a tournament.

If I could simplify what he talks about down to one key idea, it's that you must swing the clubhead. When mechanical thoughts creep into your mind, they tend to impede that process. No matter what shot you are trying to hit, you must make an effort to make a long, full backswing and give yourself enough time to coordinate your swing.

This is true of all shots, from the driver to the putter. I can't count the number of shots that I've ruined by making a short, fast backswing, especially under pressure or when you are trying to play a delicate little shot like a chip or pitch.

The most recent tournament when remembering Bob Jones's admonition helped me was in the

1990 Southwestern Bell Colonial at Colonial C.C. in Fort Worth.

I came to the par-4 17th with a three-shot lead. The wind was blowing very hard from the left to the right, and I wanted to hit a 1-iron off the tee because accuracy is so crucial. The wind is another factor that can lead you to shortening your swing, and sure enough, I came out of the shot and hung the ball way out to the right. The ball landed in a drainage ditch.

Now I had a really difficult shot. I had 172 yards to a tightly bunkered green. The wind was blowing left to right and a little bit against. I took a 4-iron, aimed it out to the left of the green, and just before I hit the ball I reminded myself to "swing the clubhead." The shot came off perfectly, and I held on to win.

NANCY LOPEZ
The 1991 Sara Lee Classic

THINK "EXTENSION"
FOR BETTER SHOTMAKING

When I'm playing in a tournament, I try not to think too much, because I become too mechanical, and I'm really very much of a feel player.

The one thing I do concentrate on is extension. When I'm taking the club back, I try to extend my arms out as far as possible, keeping my backswing "low and slow."

On the downswing I accelerate through the ball. In fact I have a great image to help me do this: I imagine that there is another ball three or four inches ahead of the real ball, and I try to hit the imaginary ball as well. This gives me great extension through the ball and toward the target.

I remember concentrating very hard on my extension when I won my last tournament of 1991, the Sara Lee Classic. I was one shot out of the lead coming into the 15th hole, a par 4. Kris Monaghan was playing ahead of me, and she bogeyed the hole. When I made a birdie, there was a two-shot swing, and I had the lead.

The next hole is a good par 5. I hit a driver from the tee, laid up short of the bunkers with a 4-wood, and then faced a tough approach into the green. The pin was cut in the back right and was sitting on a little knob. The shot is deceptive, because it plays longer than it looks. I made sure I got the ball back up the slope and made the putt for birdie. Two pars later I had the win.

Since I was four months pregnant at the time, the win was extra special, because I was pretty sure I wasn't going to have many more chances to win that year.

One other thought: when I'm under pressure, I always make sure to take a few deep breaths before I hit the shot. It gets plenty of oxygen to my brain so I can think more clearly and also helps relax my muscles—and as I get older, I need all the help relaxing that I can get.

HELEN ALFREDSSON

THE 1990 WEETABIX
BRITISH WOMEN'S OPEN

FIND YOUR KEY
AND FOCUS ON YOUR TARGET

Really good golfers have a variety of different keys or triggers that they use to help them make good swings, but I believe one thing they all have in common is their ability to really focus on the target. After all, a good swing is nice, but what really counts is hitting the ball where you need to. To do this, I think you need to pick your target and see yourself hitting that ball right at it. Once you've done that, it's a matter of keeping that focus until after you've hit the ball.

When I beat England's Jane Hill in a four-hole playoff at Woburn in 1990, my concentration was so intense that it was like I was in a trance or a zone. I could clearly see every shot, from the drive to the shortest putt, before I hit them.

Too often I see my pro-am partners get bogged down worrying about their swings, and they forget about actually playing the shot. Of course, it's important to have good, solid mechanics, but even so, I believe if you have a good, positive mental image you'll be able to hit a lot more good shots than you will if you're just preoccupied with your swing.

PETER JACOBSEN
THE 1990 BOB HOPE
CHRYSLER CLASSIC

"SOFTEN" YOUR ARMS TO REDUCE
STRESS

Like a lot of players, I've had to find a way to deal with tension and pressure on the course, particularly when I was in contention to win. If I got tense, my swing would tend to get quick and out of control. I found that if I concentrated on keeping my arms nice and soft at address it helped prevent that tension from ruining my swing. One way to do this is to grip the club very lightly, barely soling the club behind the ball. Doing this helps me make a swing controlled by the big muscles of my body rather than my arms. When you let your arms control your swing, it's very easy to get into a bad tempo.

In the 1990 Bob Hope Chrysler Classic, I came into the final round with a two-stroke lead over Mike Reid. Mike skied to a 77 on Sunday at the Palmer course at PGA West, but Brian Tennyson birdied 14, 15, and 16 to tie me for the lead. But when he missed a birdie at 18, he fell into a tie with

Scott Simpson. As I stood on the 18th tee, I knew the tournament was mine to either win or lose.

The 18th is a good finishing hole. It's a 520-yard par 5 guarded by a lake on the left. I had to hit a big drive to give myself a shot at hitting the green in two, but I also had to guard against hitting a hook into trouble. I drove the ball about 290 yards, leaving myself with about 225 yards to the front and 250 to the hole. There was a crosswind, and I had to hit a 3-iron off a downhill lie, which meant I had to guard against losing the ball to the right.

As I set up over the ball, I consciously gripped the club softly to try to keep as much tension as possible out of my swing. The ball wound up about 60 feet from the hole. I didn't have any thoughts of making the putt for an eagle. I just wanted to make sure I didn't get too cute and leave myself too much work for my birdie. I ran the putt up for a tap-in birdie and the win.

SANDY LYLE
THE 1988 MASTERS

THINK "WALTZ TIME" UNDER PRESSURE

My father taught me to play, and from the very first he always stressed the importance of tempo, particularly in tight spots during a round. He always told me that golf is a game meant to be played at waltz time, not at a quickstep. When I am playing, I try to do everything slowly. I give myself plenty of time to get to the course and warm up. I don't hurry between shots, and I try never to make a hasty decision. This is especially true when things begin to go badly. You need to act calmly and keep your wits about you, and that's hard to do if you're racing about.

In the 1988 Masters there were two holes in the final round—the 12th and 18th—where I got myself into a jam and could easily have lost the tournament by panicking. Instead I just slowed down, tried to think clearly, and played my way out of trouble.

I began the final round with a two-shot lead over my playing companion, Ben Crenshaw, and Mark Calcavecchia. I still held that lead when I came to the 155-yard par-3 12th hole—one of the most difficult par 3s in the world. The green is very narrow and is guarded by bunkers back and front. Rae's Creek flows in front of the green, waiting for any ball that hits short of the green. The pin was cut to the right side of the green, as it always is on Sunday.

Playing ahead of me in different groups, both Calcavecchia and Craig Stadler—tied at five under—had parred the 12th. I hit an 8-iron that started out right at the flag, but it began drifting to the right and came up short of the green, rolling back into the water. I stood on the tee, stunned, and tried to compose myself. I remember walking very slowly and deliberately to the drop area, taking deep breaths to try to calm my nerves and compose myself. I hit a sand wedge to the back fringe, chipped up, and made the putt for a double bogey that dropped me into a three-way tie for the lead.

Standing on the 18th tee, I decided to hit a 1-iron to avoid the bunkers guarding the left side of the landing area. I pulled the shot, and the ball wound up in the first bunker. It was a very anxious few minutes because I had no idea what kind of lie I had or what kind of shot I'd be able to play. Up ahead on the green, Calcavecchia made his par to finish at 282. I needed a par to force a playoff. I forced myself to take my time getting to the bunker, reminding myself that this, above all, was no time to hurry.

Fortunately, I had an excellent lie, far enough back from the lip of the bunker to allow me to hit a 7-iron 140 yards to the pin, which was cut on the lower level of the two-tiered green. I carried the ball some 20 feet past the hole, but once it settled it began rolling back down the slope toward the hole, stopping 10 feet above the flag. The putt never left the center of the cup, and the resulting three gave me a one-shot victory. It was the first time a player had birdied the final hole to win since Arnold Palmer beat Ken Venturi in 1960.

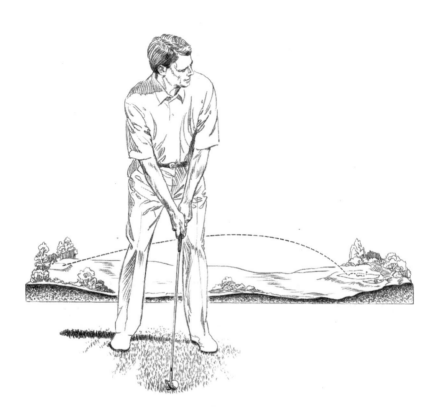

TIM SIMPSON

THE 1990 WALT DISNEY WORLD/OLDSMOBILE CLASSIC

"SEE" THE SHOT AND THEN HIT IT

The strength of my game has always been my ball striking, and when I'm playing well my swing key is to avoid swing keys altogether. I just see the target, see the shot I want to hit, and then go ahead and hit it. It's like my eyes are a camera sending a picture to my brain, and then the brain sends the message to my muscles. I've talked with athletes in other sports, like Steve Bartkowski, the former quarterback for the Falcons, and Mike Schmidt, the ex–Phillies third baseman. They say it's the same way in their sports. When you're playing well, you just act; you don't need to think about what you're going to do. The perfect example is watching a guy like Larry Bird or Michael Jordan play basketball. You know they don't have time to think of those moves, shots, or passes.

When I won the 1990 Walt Disney World/Oldsmobile Classic, it was like I was on cruise control. My mind was totally uncluttered, and everything was just so clear and vivid. I felt like there wasn't a pin I couldn't shoot at, a feeling that was helped when rains helped soften the greens in the final round. It was like the rounds Johnny Miller used to shoot in his prime or that a player like Lanny Wadkins is capable of today. In fact I had so much confidence that I had to force myself not to shoot at some sucker pin placements. I just didn't believe there could be a pin I couldn't get close to. It was a tournament when I felt that if I didn't birdie a hole it was like making a double bogey.

I led the tournament from wire to wire and wound up setting both 36- and 54-hole records. Obviously tournaments like this don't come along very often, but when they do the feeling and the confidence stay with you for a long time.

BRAD FAXON
THE 1991 BUICK OPEN

"MAINTAIN THE TRIANGLE" FOR BETTER BALL STRIKING

Coming into the final round of the 1991 Buick Open, I was five shots behind Marco Dawson and, realistically, wasn't thinking about winning. Still, I thought that if I came out firing I could make up some ground and earn a good check. I had been hitting the ball pretty well all week, mostly because of a swing thought that I had been working on for a while.

All I thought about was maintaining the triangle between my arms and upper body throughout my swing. Some people refer to this thought as remaining "connected" throughout the swing, which is also a good image to keep in mind. The idea is that your arms never swing faster than your upper body turns. This helps you maintain a good tempo throughout your swing, especially under pressure.

I came out and birdied the first two holes, which gave me a lot of confidence. I just had one of those rounds where I didn't hit many bad shots, and when I did I was able to come up with a save. That's what happened on the 12th, when I made a 10-footer to save par. I birdied 13, eagled 14, and then on 16 I had a birdie putt very similar to one I'd had there in 1983. I made the putt and then parred 18 and had to wait and see what Chip Beck did.

The playoff began on the 10th hole, which is a good, short par 4. I hit my drive into the left rough. Chip drove it right in the middle of the fairway. I had a tough angle for my approach because the pin was tucked on the left side of the green. I hit a great 9-iron to about 25 feet. Chip hit a 9-iron too, but he barely made the green. He had about a 60-footer and wound up three-putting. I got down in two and won.

ROSIE JONES
THE 1984 U.S. WOMEN'S OPEN

DON'T GET CARELESS UNDER PRESSURE

When I get under pressure and my adrenaline starts pumping, my perspective seems to change. Instead of concentrating on a specific key, my focus shifts to the shot I want to hit. I try to stay relaxed and focused on the present rather than the future or the past.

One thing I do pay a lot of attention to is my address position. When you are under pressure, it's very easy to get careless and focus on the shot before you get in a good position to hit the ball. As I set up to the ball, I check very carefully to make sure my grip and stance are in good shape. From there I just try to make sure I take the club away from the ball slowly for the first foot or so. When I jerk the club back quickly, my entire swing gets fast and I usually come over the ball and either block the ball to the right or hit a pull-hook off to the left.

As I've become more experienced, I've learned not only how to play under pressure but how to manage my game when I get in a position to win. In the 1984 Women's Open at Salem C.C. in the suburbs of Boston, I came to the last hole needing a par to tie Hollis Stacy and force a playoff, but I had been on the tour for only two years and, to be honest, didn't cope very well with the pressure.

I drove the ball into the rough and had 143 yards to the hole. The one place I couldn't afford to leave the ball was above the hole. That was death. I was between a 7-iron and an 8-iron but was unsure how the ball would fly out of the rough. I decided to try to hit an easy 7, and the ball jumped. I wound up pulling the ball 20 feet above the hole. My chip ran 30 feet past, and the bogey cost me a shot at Hollis.

The following week, at the Rochester (New York) International, I faced an almost identical situation. I came to the last hole tied with Kathy Whitworth. I had 150 yards, uphill, to the green. This time my thought pattern was totally different. I had learned that to hit a good shot under pressure you had to eliminate the negatives—the *if* and *buts* and *maybes*. At Rochester, I was able to think clearly. I knew exactly what I needed to do. I pulled a 6-iron and put the ball on the green. Two putts later I was headed for a playoff with the winningest golfer in

LPGA history. She won on the first hole, but even though I was disappointed, I was proud of the way I played.

It's a funny thing, but when I look back on the 1984 Open I wish I had won, but I realize that, at age 24, I probably wasn't mature enough to handle the responsibilities of being the Open champion.

CURT BYRUM

GET YOUR WEIGHT OVER YOUR RIGHT FOOT

Like a lot of tall players, I have a tendency to keep my weight on my left side during my swing. When I hang left like this, I wind up with a reverse weight shift, which leads me to taking the club back too much on the inside, resulting in either a hook or a blocked shot that goes weakly to the right.

I've learned that the best way for me to prevent this is to concentrate on getting my weight back on my right foot on the backswing. I don't think of anything else. My only thought at the beginning of my swing is to feel my weight move to my right heel. It naturally transfers back to my left side on the downswing.

When I first began working on this, it felt like I was swaying back and forth during the swing, but my ball striking improved dramatically, and in a short time it began to feel very comfortable.

BETH DANIEL
THE 1990 CENTEL CLASSIC

TAKE THE CLUB BACK SLOWLY

My best thoughts are basically tempo thoughts. When I'm playing well, I concentrate on swinging and playing with a good tempo, and when things start to go badly it helps if I focus on the pace of my swing, since like most people I have a tendency to get quick under pressure.

In 1990 I came to the Centel Classic at Killearn C.C. in Tallahassee at the end of one of my best years on tour. I had 18 Top-10 finishes that included seven wins. I also won my first major that year, the Mazda LPGA Championship. At Centel, I not only won the tournament but shot my low career round, a 63, in the second round.

Coming into the tournament, I was working on getting my club in the correct position at the top of my backswing. I have a tendency to get the clubface shut at the top, so I have to work on rotating my forearms like Tom Watson as I take the club back. This helps me get the clubface square to the target line instead of shut.

Once I was confident in my mechanics and that I was in good position at the top, all I worked on was my tempo, making sure I took the club back away from the ball slowly on every shot. I opened with a 71 and came back with a 63. A 68 and 69 brought me in with a 17-under-par 271, and then I had to wait and see what Nancy Lopez did on 18. She did what she very rarely does—especially on the final hole with a chance to win. She three-putted for a bogey.

DANNY EDWARDS

LIGHTEN YOUR GRIP PRESSURE
TO ERASE TENSION

I think the grip is the most underemphasized fundamental. It's the only contact a player has with the club, so how can it not be the most important element of the swing?

Players of every level—from the best pros to the worst hackers—all have a tendency to grip the club too tightly, especially under pressure. This leads to tense, tight muscles, beginning in the hands and running up through the arms and shoulders. This tension, in turn, breeds nervousness and lack of confidence, and the result is usually a swing that is short and fast.

My key under pressure—and this is something I always try to share with my pro-am partners—is to try to eliminate as much tension as possible before the shot . . . and then grip the club lightly.

KEITH CLEARWATER

TRY TO SHAPE EVERY SHOT

I have what I call "shaping thoughts" more than swing thoughts because I think it's important to try to shape every shot, one way or another. When I'm playing well, my swing is on automatic pilot. I just see the shot I want to hit and go ahead and hit it. I pick a target to aim at and then focus totally on the mental picture I have of the ball moving toward that target. If I need to draw the ball from right to left, I might focus on hitting the ball from the inside. To move it from left to right I'll concentrate on taking the clubhead away from the ball on an outside swing path.

I think that being able to confidently fade and draw the ball is also helpful because it just sharpens your concentration. If you have one basic shot that you play over and over, it's easy to get into a routine and become a little mentally sloppy. I think this little extra bit of concentration has really helped me improve my ball striking.

MIKE SOUCHAK
The 1955 Houston Open

ALWAYS HIT A FULL SHOT
UNDER PRESSURE

When I first came out on tour, I got a lot of good advice from Jackie Burke, who won 17 tournaments, including the 1956 Masters and PGA Championship. One of the things he stressed was that when you get in a position to win you must be careful not to make a mistake and beat yourself coming down the stretch.

One of those mistakes is leaving yourself half or three-quarter shots under pressure, when your nerves are tense and your mind is working rapidly. For example, let's say you have 130 yards to the hole, which might ordinarily be a nice, smooth 8-iron. Jackie taught me that in a pressure situation you're much better off trying to bust a hard 9. For one thing, your adrenaline is going to make you hit the ball farther in the first place. For another, a full shot is just easier to control than a finesse shot.

I took Jackie's advice in the closing holes of the 1955 Houston Open. I had just won at San Antonio the previous week, setting a tour scoring record. I was playing very well, but it seemed like on the last three or four holes I was between clubs on every approach shot. On the 17th I had either a good 7 or a hard 8. I hit the 8 and made a birdie. On the last hole I was between a pitching wedge and a 9-iron and went with the wedge, making par and winning by a couple shots. In every case my thought was to let it go, making sure I released the club. Too often when you try to lay off a club you wind up blocking the shot out to the right.

BOB GOALBY
THE 1968 MASTERS

LET YOUR LEFT HAND TAKE CONTROL

A swing thought that helped, in the 1968 Masters as well as in other tournaments, was this simple key: grip the club lightly but with a constant pressure in the last three fingers of your left hand. A lot of times, especially under pressure, there's a tendency to let the right hand take over. By letting the last three fingers of your left hand control the grip, you avoid the tendency to hit rather than swing—and especially hit from the top. This key also helps you swing with a good pace if you think about pushing the club back away from the ball rather than pulling it away with your right hand, which often leads to taking the club back too much to the inside.

The beauty of having a swing key that you trust is that it can help you when you're facing a shot that scares you or when you're in an unfamiliar situation. It also helps when you're playing badly and just trying to grind your way through a tough round. It may be a crutch, but sometimes a crutch is just what you need.

DOUG SANDERS
THE 1967 DORAL OPEN

CONCENTRATE ON MAKING
A LONGER SWING

The first thing you have to understand about swing keys is that they change all the time. They change as you get older because you lose some strength and flexibility. They change from day to day depending on whether you're tired or rested. They also change because you are constantly learning more about the game and your swing.

People always said I had a short swing. Well, the truth was that I had a short backswing, but my overall swing was pretty long. Still, because my backswing was so short I had to be more conscious of making as full a backswing as I could. To do this, I had two keys.

The first key was to make the fullest shoulder turn that I could. I tried to get my left shoulder behind the ball on the backswing. The second was to keep my backswing as slow as possible, because the faster I swung, the shorter my backswing became. I think those two keys would help 99.9 percent of the golfers I see.

I had a good record at Doral, winning there in 1965 and '67. One reason I played so well there is that I could handle the wind. To score well in windy conditions you have to be able to hit a lot of shots, and to do that it's crucial that you get the club in a good position at the top of your swing. In other words, you've got to complete your backswing before you can try to do something fancy with the ball.

The week I won Doral in 1967 I did a lot of visualization at night, before I went to sleep. I concentrated on my swing. I could see myself making longer and slower backswings time after time. And that week I swear that my swing was a good six inches longer than usual—and I never hit the ball better or hit a greater variety of shots.

BRUCE DEVLIN
The 1970 Alcan

GET YOUR LEFT SHOULDER UNDER YOUR CHIN FOR A BETTER TURN

Throughout my career I've had to work at being patient with my swing, especially when it came to making a full, complete backswing. The key that worked best for me was working my left shoulder under my chin on the backswing. Not only did this ensure that I'd complete my backswing, but it also helped keep me from getting too quick.

Anytime you're playing in bad weather there's a tendency to get out of your natural rhythm and become short and quick. That's why players like Sam Snead and Jack Nicklaus have always been such great bad-weather players. Their tempos never varied despite the conditions.

The 1970 Alcan tournament was played at Portmarnock in Ireland in windy, rainy conditions. Throughout the entire tournament I concentrated on completing my backswing by turning my left shoulder fully under my chin before I started my downswing. On the first day I was the only player even to break 74. I shot 65 on the second day to take a comfortable lead, and with two holes left I had a nine-shot lead. I guess you could say that was a swing key that really worked.

JANET COLES
THE 1986 S&H GOLF CLASSIC

FORCE YOURSELF TO SLOW DOWN

I'm not sure I've used mechanical swing thoughts when I've played on tour. Most of the time I just trust my swing and concentrate on my tempo. That's particularly important for me because I tend to be kind of a hyper athlete anyway, and when I'm playing well I just naturally seem to speed up my pace of play.

Ironically, one of the best final rounds I've ever played came in a tournament I didn't win. I was leading the 1986 S&H Golf Classic by three shots going into the last round. I was paired with Pat Bradley, and she was just awesome that day. She birdied the first four holes, and when we came to the fifth tee I was one shot back. I remember sitting there thinking two things. First, it was time to go flag hunting, because when Pat gets hot she very rarely beats herself. I needed to make some birdies.

Second, I told myself over and over, Take your time. Take your time. Be patient.

When it was all over, I shot a 68 for my fourth round in the 60s, but Pat was too much that day. She shot an 8-under-par 64 to beat me by a shot. I didn't win, but I sure was proud of that round.

JUDY RANKIN
The 1974 Colgate European Open

TAKE EVERYTHING BACK IN ONE PIECE

When you're playing under pressure, there's a tendency to let your arms and hands control the pace of your swing, and usually that means that you'll swing too fast and won't coordinate your arms with the rest of your body. I always tried to prevent this by taking everything—the clubhead, my hands and arms, and my upper and lower body—back in one piece. When I did that, I found I had really good rhythm and timing.

The truth is that everyone fights tension on the course, no matter how many times you've been in contention. I always struggled to get my emotions under control, and I found that if I could just find a way to relax my forearms and hands I could generally make a pretty good swing. To keep from getting jerky on the backswing, I'd try to drag the clubhead away from the ball. This would keep me from jerking the clubhead inside or cocking my wrists too early in the backswing. It would probably be imperceptible to most people, but it was something that I tried to do when the heat was on. If you study photo-graphs or films of players like Byron Nelson or Bob Jones, you'll notice they did the same thing.

I don't know if I ever accomplished this better than at Sunningdale, in England, in the 1974 Col-gate European Open. I had just gotten a new driver. It had a Penna head and a graphite shaft, which hardly anyone was playing with at the time. I was just learning to control the shaft, and I found that if I swung almost leisurely, I could really drive the ball beautifully. I never tried to force the club. I just let it do the work for me.

SCOTT HOCH
THE 1989 MASTERS

GO SLOWLY FOR THE FIRST THREE FEET

Coming into the 1989 Masters I had been playing pretty well despite driving the ball poorly. I tend to play pretty quickly, and sometimes that carries over to the pace of my swing. When I do get quick, it usually affects my driving first, and that was the case coming to Augusta.

Fortunately, I had discovered a key that was working for me. Once I set up to the ball, I took one last look at the target and then said to myself, "Slow back." It's not easy to do that, especially under pressure, but I felt that the first three feet of the swing were really the key to good timing and pace.

I opened with a 69, which left me two shots behind Lee Trevino. I skied to a 74 in the second round, but a 71 in the third round left me at 214, one shot behind Ben Crenshaw.

I played very well on Sunday, and after I birdied 15, I looked at the scoreboard and realized I had a one-shot lead. When I was coming off the 16th green, a spectator said, "Two pars to win." For some reason that caused me to lose my concentration. I just lost my focus completely. I stood on the tee, and for the first time that week I didn't consciously think about taking the club away from the ball slowly. I pushed my drive out to the right, and it hit that big tree out there, leaving me a long approach shot to a very difficult green. The ball rolled off the back of the green, and I had an almost impossible chip. I hit the best chip of my life. Then I just misread the putt. The green was wet, and the ball didn't break as much as I thought it would. I hit a good putt. It just didn't fall.

Even after the bogey on 17 I was still confident. I wasn't nervous at all. I felt my time had come. My playoff with Nick Faldo began on the 10th hole. I hit a good drive, and my approach shot wound up about 30 feet from the hole. Nick pushed his approach into the bunker and faced a tough shot. If he hit it too hard, the ball could run off the green. He played it safe, leaving himself a difficult eight-footer. I hit a good putt, leaving myself a two-footer for par. I marked the ball, and when Nick missed I had two feet left for the win. I took more time than usual over the putt, but as I prepared to hit it there was a split second of indecision. I saw it one way and hit it another. I had to hit it firmly, and it wound up four feet past the hole. It was my first three-putt of the week and just my second bogey of the day. I made the putt but lost on the next hole when Nick made a 25-footer for birdie after my pitch from off the green came up short.

ALICE MILLER

The 1985 Nabisco Dinah Shore

JUST "STAY WITH IT"

When you are under pressure, either because you're in contention to win or because you are playing badly and struggling, I think the key is to stay with your preshot routine and to keep one simple thought in mind.

A preshot routine is important because it helps with your timing and helps reduce doubt in your mind. When I watch a player and she gets out of her routine, I know she's undecided or feeling the pressure, and the chances are she's not going to pull off the shot she's trying to play. Your swing thought can be something you've used in the past, or it could be something you picked up that week or even that day. Whatever it is, stick with it as long as it's working for you. The beauty of a good swing thought is that it will not only help you make a good swing or putting stroke but will also give you something to occupy your mind. When you start thinking about a lot of different things out there, you eventually get distracted and in trouble.

I don't think I ever concentrated better in my career than I did on the final round of the 1985 Nabisco Dinah Shore at Mission Hills in Rancho Mirage, California.

I came into that round with a one-shot lead over Judy Clark (now Dickinson) and a four-shot lead over Jan Stephenson. I was playing pretty well, but Jan, whom I was paired with, was really charging. I bogeyed the 13th hole, and when we got to the par-3 14th Jan knocked it very close. The pin was cut on the back right, which is a difficult placement. I knew I needed to hit it close, not only to give myself some confidence but also to cool off Jan, who is capable of running off strings of birdies.

I was very nervous, and I just reminded myself to "stay with it." I didn't want to get quick and come out of the shot by not staying down through impact. It also helped that I consciously swung the club at about 80 percent of full speed. That helped me make good, solid contact. Anyway, I knocked the ball stiff to the pin, birdied the hole, and then two more of the last four. Jan shot a 66, but my 67 was good enough to win by three.

BOB ESTES

GO WITH YOUR "SAFE" SHOT
UNDER PRESSURE

I think a good rule for anyone is to make sure to finish the backswing on every shot, whether it's a drive or the shortest putt. If you can feel that you are finishing your backswing, it's a pretty good guarantee that you are swinging with a good tempo.

I think it's also important to have one shot—whether it's a fade or a draw—that you have a lot of confidence in. This eliminates a lot of confusion and indecision when you are under pressure, whether it's from first-tee jitters or you're in a tight spot in a match or tournament.

My safe shot is a fade. I set up with an open stance and concentrate on controlling the swing with my left hand. I try to leave my right hand out of the swing as much as possible. I aim for a spot on the left side of the landing area. If I hit the shot correctly, the ball should wind up in the middle of the fairway. If I fail to finish my backswing and hit a big slice, the ball will be in the right side of the fairway or, at the very worst, in the right rough. If the ball doesn't turn, it should still end up in the left side of the fairway.

PART II
SHORT-GAME THOUGHTS

JOEY SINDELAR
THE 1990 HARDEE'S GOLF CLASSIC

TRUST YOUR PRACTICE DRILLS— AND IMAGINATION

My father developed a practice device called a "putting board" that I've used a lot during my career. It is designed to help you keep the putter on track throughout the entire stroke.

I've found that when I have a difficult putt, if I try to imagine that I'm actually hitting the putt using the putting board, it helps take some of the pressure off and also helps me make a better stroke when my nerves and emotions are running high. So much of putting is a matter of muscle memory, and this really helps.

I can actually think of two instances when using my imagination this way really paid off. The first was at the 1985 Greater Greensboro Open, when I made an eight-footer to win. The second was the 1990 Hardee's Golf Classic, when I had to make a five-footer on the 72nd hole to tie Willie Wood and force a playoff. Both putts were just inside the right edge, which are good putts for a right-handed golfer, but the key was just imagining the board was there. It took some of the pressure off and allowed me to make a good, free stroke. I made the putt and then beat Willie in the playoff.

TOM PURTZER
THE 1991
SOUTHWESTERN BELL COLONIAL

BEND FROM THE HIPS
FOR BETTER PUTTING

One secret to good putting is getting in the right position over the ball. You want to be comfortable, but you also need to get your eyes out over the ball so you can see the line.

Coming into the Colonial, I had been experimenting a little bit with my putting setup, and I found that if I bent over from my hips I could see the line better and make a better stroke, because my arms could hang down more naturally and comfortably. I hit the ball well all week, but by making this one small adjustment in my setup I developed so much confidence in my putting that I was able to be a little more aggressive around the greens.

JIM GALLAGHER, JR.
THE 1990
GREATER MILWAUKEE OPEN

PICK A SPOT ON THE BALL

Like many other golfers, I have a tendency to follow the clubhead when I'm hitting a putt, chip, or pitch shot, which can create all kinds of problems such as either hitting the ball fat and chunking the shot or skulling the ball across the green.

I found that the best solution is to pick a specific spot on the back of the ball and concentrate very hard on the spot, not taking my eyes off it until well after the ball is gone. This not only helps prevent bad misses but also helps you make a good, quiet stroke.

This tip really helped me a lot at the 1990 Greater Milwaukee Open, when I was in contention to win my first event on tour. I had an eight-footer to save par on the 17th hole, which I made. I got into a playoff with Billy Mayfair and Ed Dogherty, which I won, largely because that putt on 17 gave me so much confidence in my short game.

JIM SIMONS
THE 1982 BING CROSBY
NATIONAL PRO-AM

TAKE A GAMBLE
IF YOU HAVE THE CONFIDENCE

I worked very hard on my chipping and pitching to prepare for the start of the 1982 season, and it paid off early, when I got into contention at the Crosby.

I was paired with Craig Stadler in the final round. On 15, the 397-yard par-4, I hit a good drive, but my 9-iron approach came up short of the right-hand bunker. The pin was cut to the back right, which is an almost impossible shot because the green slopes straight away from the hole. If I was going to get the ball close, I had to land it just over the bunker, in the fringe, in an area about the size of a sprinkler head.

I had been working on developing a sense of my backswing, trying to get a feel for just how big a backswing I needed to hit the ball a certain distance. I had had a lot of success pitching the ball that week, so I had a lot of confidence. I had played well to this point in the round, so I was on a roll.

And last but not least, I knew I had to make par, or Craig would take the lead and he might be able to run away and hide because of his power. It would give him a real edge playing the 18th, a par 5 he might be able to reach in two.

I took my time over the ball, taking enough practice swings to get the feel, then made a good, aggressive shot. The ball landed softly, right on the spot I was aiming at, and came to rest three feet from the hole. I'd like to be able to say I made the putt, but it was so fast that I missed it and left myself a six-footer coming back up the hill. I made the putt and went on to birdie the par-3 17th, which Craig bogeyed to give me a two-shot cushion, which was the winning margin.

JIM SIMONS
THE 1978 MEMORIAL TOURNAMENT

SEE THE SHOT . . . THEN PRACTICE IT

When I came into the final hole of the 1978 Memorial at the difficult Muirfield Village golf course, I needed to make a par to beat Billy Kratzert by a shot. I hit a good drive, but my second shot missed the green to the left, which is dead. The pin was cut halfway back and to the left side of the green. From my lie I could just barely see the top of the flag, which made the shot even tougher.

This was one of those shots that's made even more difficult because you never really can practice it. The only way I could hope to get it close was to completely visualize the shot: how high I had to get the ball into the air, where I had to land it, how much it was going to break, and how fast it would run once it landed.

Once I had visualized the shot, I tried to get a feel for the type of swing I had to make and how hard I had to hit the ball. To do this I must have made six or more practice swings, trying to feel exactly what the swing should be like. Once I had that feeling, I went ahead and played the shot.

I hit the best shot I could possibly play, and the ball still ran 21 feet past the hole. I made the putt coming back and had my second win on tour.

COREY PAVIN
THE 1991 BOB HOPE
CHRYSLER CLASSIC

THINK ABOUT THE LINE—
NOT THE SPEED—OF THE PUTT

In the 1991 Bob Hope, I had a five-foot putt that I needed to make to give me a chance to get into a playoff with Mark O'Meara. Mark had birdied the second and fifth holes to take a four-shot lead, but I was able to birdie the sixth, seventh, eighth, and ninth holes to pull back to even.

The putt I faced on 18 to get into the playoff was difficult. I needed to start the ball just inside the right edge of the cup. When I'm in a situation like that, I focus totally on the line. When there's that kind of pressure, you need to think as clearly as possible. I've found that I can't do that if I'm thinking about both the line and the speed of the putt.

I think the time to work on your touch is before the round or when you're practicing. Take that feel with you to the course and then concentrate on getting the ball started on the right line. The speed will take care of itself. It did for me at the Hope. I made the putt and went on to win the playoff with Mark when I pitched in from the rough short of the green.

CHIP BECK

THINK "1-2," SMOOTH AND STEADY

When I've putted well, I've tended to have two key thoughts. The first is to putt to a "1-2" rhythm, similar to the sound of a grandfather clock.

The second thought is to be smooth and steady throughout the stroke. It's especially important to be steady right to the very end of the stroke. This helps ensure that you won't decelerate at impact, which leads to a weak stroke.

LYNN CONNELLY

THE 1990
ORIX HAWAIIAN LADIES OPEN

LET YOUR LEFT HAND
CONTROL THE STROKE

A key to good putting is to find a way to prevent your wrists from breaking down at impact. The best way I've found to do this is to maintain a constant pressure with the last three fingers of my left hand and let that hand control the entire stroke. Too often I see players let their right hand take over, and the result is a loose, flippy stroke that isn't very consistent.

Putting is the great equalizer. When you're hitting the ball badly, it can keep you alive. That was the case for me in Hawaii in 1990. I was all over the place from tee to green, but from 10 in I felt like I couldn't miss. I opened with a 69, soared to a 75 in the second round, and then held it all together with a 73 in the last round to finish at 217, seven shots back.

KAY COCKERILL
The 1991 LPGA Bay State Classic

STAY RELAXED OVER THE PUTT

When I'm putting well, it seems like all I have to do is pick out the line and then just try to stay relaxed with my hands, shoulders, and arms over the ball. When I get tight, it's very difficult for me to make short putts or to get longer-approach putts close to the hole, because the tension and pressure make it very hard to have any feel. The key is keeping your hands very soft throughout the stroke, because as soon as you begin to tighten your grip on the club the tension rises through your arms and into your shoulders. Once this happens, it's tough to make a smooth, consistent stroke.

I shared the lead with Caroline Keggi after 54 holes and was pretty relaxed going into the final round. I putted very well just because I was so relaxed and made a lot of really difficult two-putts until the final three holes, when I began to get a little nervous and tight. Still, I finished third, which was my best finish on tour to that point.

DONNA CAPONI
The 1981 LPGA Championship

RELEASE THE PUTTERHEAD

Dave Stockton, the 1991 Ryder Cup captain and winner of two PGA Championships, is one of my best friends and favorite golf partners. He's also one of the best putters that ever played the game, so when he gives me advice I make sure that I pay attention.

He's always told me to "release the putterhead" through the stroke, especially under pressure, when the tendency is to hold on and block the putt without much authority.

In the 1981 LPGA Championship at Kings Island, I came to the final green in a three-way tie with 1979 U.S. Women's Open champion Jerilyn Britz and Pat Meyers. I had about a 15-footer to win, and I looked at it from every possible angle. No matter how many times I looked at it, it always looked dead straight. In that situation it's hard to bring yourself to believe that any putt is that straight. At the time I was using an old Ray Cook mallet putter that Dave had given me. He had used it to win the 1976 PGA Championship at Congressional. I looked at the putter and remembered Dave's advice. I said to myself, "OK, Dave, release the putterhead." I aimed it right in the center of the hole and put a beautiful stroke on the ball. It dropped in, and I had won my fifth major championship.

PART III
COURSE STRATEGY THOUGHTS

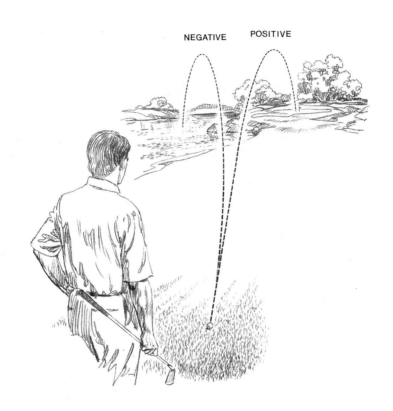

GARY McCORD
WHATEVER YOUR THOUGHT, MAKE IT POSITIVE

The key to a good swing thought is finding one that will occupy your brain with positive thoughts for the one second it takes to hit a shot. That's why visualization is so important. Every shot should have a shape to it, which you can see in your imagination and then try to actually hit. Your muscles work best when they are reacting to a positive image and plan. The more you can concentrate on the positives, the better off you'll be.

Here's a perfect example: Let's say you're facing a shot to a green that's guarded by water on the left. If you say to yourself, "Whatever you do, don't hit it left," guess where your ball is heading? Dead left most of the time. Negative images and thoughts produce negative results. But if you say, "OK, let's just start it out to the right and try to draw it back into the green," bingo! Your brain gave your body a chance. See, it's a simple game. Right.

ANDREW MAGEE
The 1991 Hertz Bay Hill Classic

TRUST YOUR FIRST THOUGHT

There's an old saying, "Your first instincts are usually the right instincts," and I think that definitely applies to golf. More often than not, when you look at a putt, the first line that you see is usually the right one. What happens is that golfers—both good and not so good—manage to think their way into a mistake.

I think that's especially true when you are facing a difficult shot. You instinctively visualize the shot you want to play, but a lot of times you talk yourself out of the shot and into playing a different one—one you might not be as comfortable with.

When I came to the 16th hole at Bay Hill in the third round, I knew I had to make something happen. I hit a pretty good drive, but then we had a long wait. As I stood in the fairway, I considered my options: My first instinct was to take a 3-iron and try to hit it up over some trees with a fade, hoping to reach the green in two and have a putt for an eagle. That was risky, though. I could have hit the ball into the trees; or, even worse, I could have dumped the ball into the water that fronts the green. The safer option was to lay up with a 7-iron, then play a wedge into the green and take a run at a birdie.

The more I thought about it, the more uncomfortable I became, because the indecision was starting to work on my confidence and concentration. Finally I grabbed my 3-iron and hit the shot just the way I had planned. I made the putt for the eagle, finished the round with a two-shot lead, and then won the title when the next day's round was rained out.

When I talk about trusting your first thought on a shot, I'm not suggesting that you make a rash decision. It's important to consider all the options before you pull the club out of your bag, but just think back over your rounds—about the shots that worked and the ones that didn't. I'll bet you find that when you trusted your instincts you hit the best shots.

KATHY WHITWORTH

NEVER KID YOURSELF

Harvey Penick, my longtime teacher, had a wonderful piece of advice for his pupils when they were heading out to play in a tournament. It was very simple: "Take dead aim." In other words, keep your mind focused on your work.

I've always been a percentage player, and it has paid off in my share of wins (88). To me the key was being able to control the ball. I never wanted to make wild swings or try a shot I didn't honestly feel I could make. I read or hear about players who try to talk themselves into a shot by telling themselves they're good players or good ball strikers or whatever. I just don't believe you can kid yourself that way. I think that when you go against the odds and try to hit a shot you're not comfortable with, all you're doing is putting added pressure on yourself. For example, if you suffer from first-tee jitters—and who doesn't?—telling yourself that you're a great driver isn't going to help you get the ball airborne, but a fairway wood might. Again, you've got to play the percentages and be honest with yourself.

I think it's also important to realize that you and your game are going to change from day to day. Just because you were able to hit a certain shot one day doesn't mean you'll be able to hit it at will. Plus, you have to be honest enough with yourself to know how you are really going to react in a certain situation.

Finally, when you get in a position to win a match or a tournament, you've got to tell yourself that it's yours to win or lose and then do whatever you have to do to avoid beating yourself.

MARK BROOKS

HIT IT HARD UNDER PRESSURE

One thing I've learned on tour is not to try to get cute under pressure. When the heat is on, you want to go ahead and play a good, full shot rather than try something fancy. If that means playing to the center of a green rather than trying to cut the ball into a tight pin, then you've got to play the percentages and go with the safer shot.

The same is true when you find yourself in between clubs facing, for example, either a hard 6-iron or an easy 5. In that case I'll definitely go with the hard 6 because it will let me make a good, full swing and accelerate the club through the hitting area. Too often, when you try to take a little something off the shot, you cut off your backswing and get out of tempo.

Another reason for hitting the shorter club is that, on a lot of courses, the real trouble is to the sides of the green and over the green. If you come up a little short, you are generally playing back up to the hole and can usually salvage par. Miss most greens anyplace else, and you're looking at a bogey—or worse.

HAL SUTTON

The 1986 Memorial Tournament

NARROW YOUR FOCUS UNDER PRESSURE

In the 1986 Memorial I found myself in a duel with Jack Nicklaus in his own tournament in his own backyard. In the last round Jack lit the place up, making six or seven birdies. With every birdie the crowd got more and more into it, and the roars got louder and louder. When you're in that position, it's very easy to get nervous and lose your focus.

As the pressure began to heat up, I came up with a little something to help me cope with it. I found that if I concentrated very intensely on a single blade of grass, it helped me block out the crowd and all the other distractions. It wasn't something I'd ever done before or even had heard about, but it worked beautifully, especially on the greens, when I had more time between shots and the gallery was closer.

I'm not sure that concentrating that hard is something you can do all the time or whether you should even try. That may be asking too much of anyone. Still, sometimes you need something to take your mind off the pressure, and that time around it worked for me.

197

AMY ALCOTT
The 1976 LPGA Classic

SOMETIMES YOU JUST HAVE TO GET ANGRY

When I first came out on tour, one of my sponsors, Bob Williams, told me a story that I'll never forget.

One year Bob was following Ben Hogan at the Los Angeles Open at Riviera. Walking alongside Hogan was a reporter who peppered Hogan with one question after another. Finally Hogan turned to the man, his steely blue eyes narrowing, and said, "Damn it, Jack. Do you have to ask me everything?"

After his round, Hogan explained to Bob why he'd lost his temper with the reporter.

"Sometimes," Hogan said, "you just have to get mad at something or someone to take the pressure off."

In 1976 I was in a position to win my second tournament on tour, the LPGA Classic at Forsgate C.C. in New Jersey. I had won in my rookie year, but I was still uncomfortable near the lead. I was paired with Jane Blalock, and we came to the final hole tied for the lead. Jane was playing the best golf of her career, and she was always a tough person to beat.

Jane drove her ball into the rough, then played her second shot 25 feet past the hole. Now it was my turn, and I was so nervous I was literally shaking. If there was ever a time to choke, this was it.

Standing there in the fairway, I remembered Bob's Hogan story and decided to try it out.

"Damn it," I said under my breath. "I'm a good player, and I can beat Jane on her best day. I've got 146 to the hole, and I know just the shot I need to play."

I took out a 6-iron and hit my favorite shot, a little knockdown that cut in there about six feet below the hole. My stroke wasn't the smoothest you ever saw, but the ball fell in the left side of the cup, and I had my second win.

I'm not suggesting you get so mad that steam starts hissing out of your ears, but a little anger can help focus your attention nicely.

TAMMIE GREEN
The 1989 du Maurier Classic

PLAY TOTALLY RELAXED
AND WITHOUT FEAR

I try very hard not to put extra pressure on myself during a round, but pressure is a reality when you play tournament golf. Sometimes it comes when you get near the lead in a tournament. Sometimes it comes when you're playing badly. Other times it comes when you're playing good golf but you can't make anything happen.

At the start of the 1989 du Maurier, I wrote myself a message on a slip of paper. It said, "Play totally relaxed and without fear." The whole idea was to do whatever I could to keep the pressure off. My caddie, Jimmy Gilmour, had me sign the note, and he kept it with him all week. I trailed Betsy King by a shot after the first two rounds and then took the lead on Saturday with a 70 while Betsy skied to a 74.

I went into Sunday's round leading the tournament, which was a new experience for me. I was nervous, but I was determined to go out, make some birdies, and have some fun. Pat Bradley came out and eagled the sixth hole to pull within a shot, but I came back and eagled it a few minutes later. Then I birdied number seven. Nancy Lopez came along and birdied 12 to move within a shot, and then I did the same thing to give myself a little better cushion.

Through all of this, Jimmy kept pulling the paper out and forcing me to read it. I'd kick back, laugh, and say, "Yeah, Jimmy, it's worked so far," and I'd keep going. It helped a lot to take deep breaths. A lot of times, under pressure, you forget to breathe properly, and as a result you can't think clearly. On the last five holes I took plenty of deep breaths and trusted my instincts. Whatever shot I visualized first was the one I went out there and hit. And I tried very hard not to second-guess myself.

SALLY LITTLE

PLAY WITHIN YOURSELF

I've always had very good mechanics, so I've never felt the need to rely on specific swing thoughts, although I do believe they can be very helpful. As a result, under pressure I always go back and make sure my grip and alignment are correct, and then I try to take the club away from the ball slowly and swing with a good tempo.

In each of my 15 tour wins I've focused on playing within myself. I don't try anything fancy, just concentrating on hitting fairways and greens, and I always play to the center of both whenever possible.

I also try to play in the present tense. Very often, when people get in a position to win a match or a tournament they begin thinking about everything except getting the job done. They think about the remaining holes, the money, or getting their name on a trophy. And the opposite is often true. If you have a good hole or a bad hole, it's important to avoid dwelling on the past. The truth of the matter is you can't control the past or the future. All you can deal with is the job at hand—as well as you can.

JIM HALLET

THE 1991 BANK OF BOSTON CLASSIC

BE SURE YOU'RE RIGHT, THEN GO AHEAD

In the final round of the 1991 Bank of Boston Classic, I drove the ball into the thick rough on the 17th hole. The 17th is a good hole with a green guarded by water.

I had 170 yards to the hole, and after I sized up the lie, the wind, and my position in the field, I decided I could get a 5-iron to the green. The problem was that my caddy—who also happened to be my father—wanted me to lay up with a wedge short of the water and then play another wedge into the green and play for a one-putt par.

We went back and forth for a while before I decided to go ahead and trust my first instinct and hit the 5-iron. I wanted to fade the ball, so I took the club back outside the line and hung on with my left hand at impact, not letting the clubface turn over. The shot turned out perfectly, and I finished par-birdie and picked up a good check.

The lesson here isn't that you should ignore your father, or even your caddy, but that you've got to have the confidence to trust your first reaction and play the shot you want to play, even if it means taking a gamble.

JIM THORPE

LEAVE YOURSELF A DOWNHILL PUTT UNDER PRESSURE

Anytime you are in a tight match, I think it's a good idea to try to leave yourself a downhill putt, because that way you don't have to worry very much about the speed of the putt. All you have to do is give it a good read, pick the spot you want to start the ball out over, and then just get the ball started rolling toward the hole.

To do this, you have to think backward. In other words, when you're out there in the fairway, make sure you take enough club to get the ball to the hole. Who knows? Maybe you'll get lucky and hole out your approach shot.

BOBBY NICHOLS

DON'T GET DOWN ON YOURSELF

When I'm playing well, I seem to do things almost by instinct. I might think "Tempo" or "Keep it slow," but I very rarely have any mechanical thoughts.

When I'm playing badly, like anyone else I get doubts and uncertainties. If those linger, there's just no way I'm going to turn things around and begin playing better. The best thing to do is just try to have patience and work hard. It's tough when you keep struggling and still come up empty. It's very easy to get down on yourself, but I think it helps if you remember that nobody ever claimed golf was a fair game. Some days the breaks go all your way, and other times you can't buy any luck. After winning 11 times on the regular tour and once on the senior tour, I believe everything evens out in the long run. I think all the best players have that kind of attitude. It's the only way I know to keep on an even keel during a round or during a tournament.

MEG MALLON
THE 1991 U.S. WOMEN'S OPEN

LET YOUR ABILITY TAKE OVER

When I came to the final hole of the U.S. Women's Open at Colonial C.C., I remember having the same thought I had earlier in the year when I won the Mazda LPGA Championship and the Oldsmobile Classic—all I wanted to do was let my natural ability take over.

When you get in a position to win, or find yourself under pressure, you're much better off if you can relax and not try to force something to happen. I tell myself, "You've prepared for this your entire career. You've hit this shot 1,000 times. Now just hit it." Of course, the truth is you had better honestly be prepared. If you haven't practiced the shot often enough to really be ready, all the pep talks in the world won't help. You can't kid yourself into becoming a good player in the clutch.

It also helps to know your game and yourself. I tend to focus better under pressure, which is a big plus. I know that sometimes my swing gets a little lazy, or loopy, when I'm not concentrating. But when

the adrenaline kicks in, my swing becomes more solid and compact, and my ball striking really improves.

Coming into the final round of the Open, I was two shots behind Pat Bradley and Joan Pitcock. I got off to a good start, and while I knew I was in contention, I really didn't want to know where I stood. Thinking about the leaderboard would only hurt my concentration and increase the pressure— and I didn't need any more pressure on me at that point. I birdied 11, 14, and 15, and as I stood on the 16th tee a spectator told me I had the lead. That's when I tried to focus on staying calm and letting my natural ability take over.

On 16 I ran my birdie putt $3\frac{1}{2}$ feet past and had a tough downhill putt coming back. Looking back, holing that was the putt of the tournament because it gave me a boost that got me through the final two holes.

BOB GOALBY
The 1968 Masters

LEARN TO BELIEVE IN YOURSELF

Sam Snead gave me a great piece of advice one time. He said that when you get in a position to win a tournament, instead of being nervous you should realize that the reason you're in that position in the first place is that you're a good player. And since you're a good player, you should make the most of the situation. I guess if anyone should know, it should be Sam.

By the time I came to the 1968 Masters, I had already won several times on tour and had played well in some majors. Still, playing the final nine holes at Augusta on Sunday in a position to win really put the heat on. Remembering Sam's advice helped a lot.